The Meditation Handbook

The Meditation Handbook is a practical guide to meditation. It teaches us how to make both ourself and others happy. Although we wish to be happy all the time, we do not know how to be, and because of this we usually destroy the happiness we have by developing anger and other delusions.

The Meditation Handbook

MEDITATIONS TO MAKE OUR LIFE HAPPY AND MEANINGFUL

GESHE KELSANG GYATSO

New Age Books

ISBN: 978-81-7822-066-6

Second Revised Edition: 2007
First NAB Edition: 2002

In association with Tharpa Publications, Conishead Priory,
Ulverston, Cumbria LA12 9QQ, England

Frontispiece of Buddha Shakyamuni by Chating Jamyang Lama.
Line illustrations from the Wheel of Life.
Photographs depict the eight auspicious symbols.

Published by
NEW AGE BOOKS
A-44 Naraina Industrial Area, Phase-I
New Delhi 110 028
INDIA
Email: nab@vsnl.in
Website: www.newagebooksindia.com

Printed in India
at Shri Jainendra Press
A-45 Naraina Industrial Area, Phase-I
New Delhi 110 028
INDIA

Contents

THE GREAT SCOPE

Preface

Buddha, the founder of Buddhism, appeared in this world in 624 BC. Just as doctors give different medicine for people with different illnesses, so Buddha gave different teachings for people with different problems and capacities. In all, he gave 84,000 different types of teaching, or Dharma. One of the most important of these is the *Perfection of Wisdom Sutra,* which in Tibetan has twelve volumes translated from Sanskrit. To help us understand how to integrate these teachings into our daily life, the Buddhist Master Atisha wrote *Lamp for the Path to Enlightenment*, also known as the *Stages of the Path*, or *Lamrim* in Tibetan. Although short, this text contains the entire meaning of the *Perfection of Wisdom Sutra*.

Later, the Tibetan Buddhist Master Je Tsongkhapa wrote extensive, middling, and condensed commentaries to Atisha's Lamrim teachings. I have prepared this new meditation handbook based on Je Tsongkhapa's Lamrim commentaries. The purpose of doing this is to make it easier for people of the modern world to understand and practise this precious holy Dharma known as "Kadam Lamrim". Part One of this book presents the basic foundation of the path to enlightenment, and Part Two presents the actual path to enlightenment. Detailed explanations can be found in the books *Transform Your Life* and *Joyful Path of Good Fortune*.

If you read this book sincerely with a good motivation free from negative views, I guarantee that you will receive great benefit for your daily happiness.

Geshe Kelsang Gyatso,
USA,
March 2003.

PART ONE

Foundation

Follow the path to enlightenment

INTRODUCTION

The New Meditation Handbook is a practical guide to meditation. It teaches us how to make both ourself and others happy. Although we wish to be happy all the time, we do not know how to be, and because of this we usually destroy the happiness we have by developing anger and other delusions. As the Buddhist Master Shantideva says:

> ... although they wish for happiness,
> Out of ignorance they destroy it like a foe.

We believe that by simply improving external conditions, we can be truly happy. Motivated by this belief, most countries have made remarkable material progress. However, as we can see, this does not really make us happier or reduce our problems but instead creates more problems, suffering, and danger. Because we have polluted our environment, water, and air, physically we are becoming more unhealthy, and different diseases are spreading throughout the world. Our lives are now more complicated, and mentally we are becoming more unhappy and worried. There are now more problems and greater dangers than ever before. This shows that we cannot make ourself happy by simply improving external conditions. Of course we need basic human conditions because we are human beings, but external conditions can only make us happy if our mind is peaceful. If our mind is not peaceful, we shall never be happy, even if our external conditions are perfect. For example, when we are enjoying ourself with our friends at a party, if we become angry for some particular reason, the moment we get angry our happiness disappears. This is because anger has destroyed our inner peace, or mental peace.

Without inner peace, there is no real happiness at all. The more we control our mind, the more our inner peace increases and the happier we become. Therefore, the real method to make ourself happy is to control our own mind. By controlling our mind – in particular, our anger, our attachment, and especially our self-grasping – all of our problems will disappear. We shall experience deep inner peace and be happy all the time. Problems, suffering, and unhappiness do not exist outside the mind; they are feelings and thus part of our mind. Therefore, it is only by controlling our mind that we can permanently stop our problems and make ourself and others truly happy.

The meditation practices presented in this book are actual methods to control our mind. Because everyone has different wishes and capacities, many different levels of meditation practice are given. In the beginning we should choose the level we feel most comfortable with, and gradually, through improving our understanding and familiarity, advance progressively to the higher levels. By continuously engaging in these meditations with joy and patience, we shall accomplish the ultimate goal of human life.

What is the ultimate goal of human life? What is it that we feel is most important for our happiness? Is it having a more attractive body, or lots of money and a good reputation, or fame and power, or excitement and adventure? We may feel that if we could only find the right place to live, the right possessions, the right work, the right friends, the right partner – the right everything – we would be truly happy.

Consequently, we put most of our time and energy into trying to rearrange our world so as to achieve these aims. Sometimes this works, but only up to a point, and only for a short while. No matter how successful we are in creating seemingly perfect external conditions, there are invariably drawbacks; they can never give us the perfect lasting happiness that all of us long for. If we have made seeking happiness from external conditions the principal meaning of our life, eventually we shall be deceived, as none of them can help us at the time of our death. As an end in themselves, worldly attainments are hollow – they are not the real essence of human life.

In the past when human beings had more abundant merit, it is said that there were wish-granting jewels that had the power to grant wishes. But even these most precious worldly possessions could only fulfil wishes for contaminated happiness – they could never bestow the pure happiness that comes from a pure mind. Moreover, these wish-granting jewels only had the power to grant wishes in one life and could not protect their owners in future lives, so ultimately even they were deceptive.

Only the attainment of full enlightenment will never deceive us. What is enlightenment? It is omniscient wisdom free from all mistaken appearances. A person who possesses this wisdom is an enlightened being, a "Buddha". All beings other than Buddhas experience mistaken appearances all the time, day and night, even during sleep.

Whatever appears to us, we perceive as existing from its own side. This is mistaken appearance. We perceive "I" and "mine" as existing from their own side, and our mind grasps strongly at this appearance, believing it to be true – this is the mind of self-grasping ignorance. Due to this, we perform many inappropriate actions that lead us to experience suffering. This is the fundamental reason why we suffer. Enlightened beings are completely free from mistaken appearances and the sufferings they produce.

It is only by attaining enlightenment that we can fulfil our deepest wish for pure and lasting happiness, for nothing in this impure world has the power to fulfil this wish. Only when we become a fully enlightened Buddha shall we experience the profound and lasting peace that comes from a permanent cessation of all delusions and their imprints. We shall be free from all faults and mental obscurations, and possess the qualities needed to help all living beings directly. We shall then be an object of refuge for all living beings.

Through this understanding, we can clearly see that the attainment of enlightenment is the ultimate goal and real meaning of our precious human life. Since our main wish is to be happy all the time and to be completely free from all faults and suffering, we must develop the strong intention to attain enlightenment. We should think, "I need to attain enlightenment because in this impure world there is no real happiness anywhere."

WHAT IS MEDITATION?

Meditation is a mind that concentrates on a virtuous object, and which is the main cause of mental peace. The practice of meditation is a method for acquainting our mind with virtue. The more familiar our mind is with virtue, the calmer and more peaceful it becomes. When our mind is peaceful, we are free from worries and mental discomfort, and we experience true happiness. If we train our mind to become peaceful we shall be happy all the time, even in the most adverse conditions; but if our mind is not peaceful, then even if we have the most pleasant external conditions we shall not be happy. Therefore, it is important to train our mind through meditation.

Whenever we meditate, we are performing an action that causes us to experience inner peace in the future. Day and night, throughout our life, we usually experience delusions, which are the opposite to mental peace. However, sometimes we naturally experience inner peace. This is because in our previous lives we concentrated on virtuous objects. A virtuous object is one that causes us to develop a peaceful mind when we concentrate on it. If we concentrate on an object that causes us to develop an unpeaceful mind, such as anger or attachment, this indicates that for us the object is non-virtuous. There are also many neutral objects that are neither virtuous nor non-virtuous.

There are two types of meditation: analytical meditation and placement meditation. Analytical meditation involves contemplating the meaning of a spiritual instruction that we have heard or read. By contemplating such instructions deeply, eventually we reach a definite conclusion or cause a specific virtuous state of mind to arise. This is the object of placement meditation. We then concentrate single-pointedly on this conclusion or virtuous state of mind for as long

Cut the root of suffering

as possible to become deeply acquainted with it. This single-pointed concentration is placement meditation. Often, analytical meditation is called "contemplation" and placement meditation is called "meditation". Placement meditation depends upon analytical meditation, and analytical meditation depends upon listening to or reading spiritual instructions.

THE BENEFITS OF MEDITATION

The purpose of meditation is to make our mind calm and peaceful. As mentioned earlier, if our mind is peaceful we shall be free from worries and mental discomfort, and so we shall experience true happiness; but if our mind is not peaceful, we shall find it very difficult to be happy, even if we are living in the very best conditions. If we train in meditation, our mind will gradually become more and more peaceful, and we shall experience a purer and purer form of happiness. Eventually we shall be able to stay happy all the time, even in the most difficult circumstances.

Usually we find it difficult to control our mind. It seems as if our mind is like a balloon in the wind – blown here and there by external circumstances. If things go well, our mind is happy, but if they go badly, it immediately becomes unhappy. For example, if we get what we want, such as a new possession, a new position, or a new partner, we become excited and cling to it tightly. However, since we cannot have everything we want, and since we shall inevitably be separated from the friends, position, and possessions we currently enjoy, this mental stickiness, or attachment, serves only to cause us pain. On the other hand, if we do not get what we want, or if we lose something that we like, we become despondent or irritated. For example, if we are forced to work with a colleague whom we dislike, we shall probably become irritated and feel aggrieved, with the result that we shall be unable to work with him or her efficiently and our time at work will become stressful and unrewarding.

Such fluctuations of mood arise because we are too closely involved in the external situation. We are like a child making a sandcastle who is excited when it is first made, but who becomes upset when it is destroyed by the incoming tide. By training in meditation, we create an inner space and clarity that enables us to control our mind regardless of the external circumstances. Gradually we develop mental equilibrium, a balanced mind that is happy all the time, rather than an unbalanced mind that oscillates between the extremes of excitement and despondency.

If we train in meditation systematically, eventually we shall be able to eradicate from our mind the delusions that are the causes of all our problems and suffering. In this way, we shall come to experience permanent inner peace. Then, day and night in life after life, we shall experience only peace and happiness.

At the beginning, even if our meditation does not seem to be going well, we should remember that simply by applying effort to training in meditation, we are creating the mental karma to experience inner peace in the future. The happiness of this life and of our future lives depends upon the experience of inner peace, which in turn depends upon the mental action of meditation. Since inner peace is the source of all happiness, we can see how important meditation is.

HOW TO BEGIN MEDITATION

The first stage of meditation is to stop distractions and make our mind clearer and more lucid. This can be accomplished by practising a simple breathing meditation. We choose a quiet place to meditate and sit in a comfortable position. We can sit in the traditional cross-legged posture or in any other position that is comfortable. If we wish, we can sit in a chair. The most important thing is to keep our back straight to prevent our mind from becoming sluggish or sleepy.

We sit with our eyes partially closed and turn our attention to our breathing. We breathe naturally, preferably through the nostrils, without attempting to control our breath, and we try to become aware of the sensation of the breath as it enters and leaves the nostrils. This sensation is our object of meditation. We should try to concentrate on it to the exclusion of everything else.

At first our mind will be very busy, and we might even feel that the meditation is making our mind busier; but in reality we are just becoming more aware of how busy our mind actually is. There will be a great temptation to follow the different thoughts as they arise, but we should resist this and remain focused single-pointedly on the sensation of the breath. If we discover that our mind has wandered and is following our thoughts, we should immediately return it to the breath. We should repeat this as many times as necessary until the mind settles on the breath.

If we practise patiently in this way, gradually our distracting thoughts will subside and we shall experience a sense of inner peace and relaxation. Our mind will feel lucid and spacious and we shall feel refreshed. When the sea is rough, sediment is churned up and the water becomes murky, but when the wind dies down the mud gradually settles and the water becomes clear. In a similar way, when the otherwise incessant flow of our distracting thoughts is calmed through concentrating on the breath, our mind becomes unusually lucid and clear. We should stay with this state of mental calm for a while.

Even though breathing meditation is only a preliminary stage of meditation, it can be quite powerful. We can see from this practice that it is possible to experience inner peace and contentment just by controlling the mind, without having to depend at all upon external conditions. When the turbulence of distracting thoughts subsides and our mind becomes still, a deep happiness and contentment naturally arises from within. This feeling of contentment and well-being helps us to cope with the busyness and difficulties of daily life. So much of the stress and tension we normally experience comes from our mind, and many of the problems we experience, including ill health, are caused or aggravated by this stress. Just by doing breathing meditation for ten or fifteen minutes each day, we shall be able to reduce this stress. We shall experience a calm, spacious feeling in the mind, and many of our usual problems will fall away. Difficult situations will become easier to deal with, we shall naturally feel warm and well disposed towards other people, and our relationships with others will gradually improve.

We should train in this preliminary meditation until we reduce our gross distractions, and then train in the twenty-one meditations explained in *The New Meditation Handbook*. When we do these meditations, we begin by calming the mind with breathing meditation as just explained, and then we proceed to the stages of analytical and placement meditation according to the specific instructions for each meditation.

BACKGROUND KNOWLEDGE REQUIRED FOR MEDITATION

Since the meditations presented in this book assume a belief in rebirth, or reincarnation, and in karma, or actions, a brief description of the process of death and rebirth, and the places in which we can be reborn, may be helpful.

The mind is neither physical, nor a by-product of physical processes, but is a formless continuum that is a separate entity from the body. When the body disintegrates at death, the mind does not cease. Although our superficial conscious mind ceases, it does so by dissolving into a deeper level of consciousness, the very subtle mind; and the continuum of the very subtle mind has no beginning and no end. It is this mind that, when thoroughly purified, transforms into the omniscient mind of a Buddha.

Every action we perform leaves an imprint on our very subtle mind, and each imprint eventually gives rise to its own effect. Our mind is like a field, and performing actions is like sowing seeds in that field. Virtuous actions sow seeds of future happiness and non-virtuous actions sow seeds of future suffering. The seeds we have sown in the past remain dormant until the conditions necessary for their germination come together. In some cases, this can be many lifetimes after the original action was performed.

The seeds that ripen when we die are very important because they determine what kind of rebirth we shall take. Which particular seed ripens at death depends upon the state of mind in which we die. If we die with a peaceful mind, this will stimulate a virtuous seed and we shall take a fortunate rebirth; but if we die with an unpeaceful mind, in a state of anger, say, this will stimulate a non-virtuous seed and we shall take an unfortunate rebirth. This is similar to the way in which nightmares are triggered off by our being in an agitated state of mind just before falling asleep.

The analogy of falling asleep is not accidental, for the process of sleeping, dreaming, and waking closely resembles the process of death, intermediate state, and rebirth. When we fall asleep, our gross inner winds gather and dissolve inwards, and our mind becomes progressively more and more subtle until it transforms into the very subtle mind of the clear light of sleep. While the clear light of sleep is manifest, we experience deep sleep, and to others we resemble a dead person. When it ends, our mind becomes gradually more and more gross and we pass through the various levels of the dream state. Finally, our normal powers of memory and mental control are restored and we wake up. When this happens, our dream world disappears and we perceive the world of the waking state.

A very similar process occurs when we die. As we die, our winds dissolve inwards and our mind becomes progressively more and more subtle until the very subtle mind of the clear light of death becomes manifest. The experience of the clear light of death is very similar to the experience of deep sleep. After the clear light of death has ceased, we experience the stages of the intermediate state, or "bardo" in Tibetan, which is a dream-like state that occurs between death and rebirth. After a few days or weeks, the intermediate state ends and we take rebirth. Just as, when we wake from sleep, the dream world disappears and we perceive the world of the waking state, so, when we take rebirth, the appearances of the intermediate state cease and we perceive the world of our next life.

The only significant difference between the process of sleeping, dreaming, and waking and the process of death, intermediate state, and rebirth is that after the clear light of sleep has ceased, the relationship between our mind and our present body remains intact, whereas after the clear light of death, this relationship is broken.

While we are in the intermediate state, we experience different visions that arise from the karmic seeds that were activated immediately before death. If negative seeds were activated, these visions will be nightmarish, but if positive seeds were activated, they will be predominantly pleasant.

In either case, once the karmic seeds have matured sufficiently, they impel us to take rebirth in one or other of the six realms of samsara.

The six realms are actual places in which we can be reborn. They are brought into existence through the power of our actions, or karma. There are three types of action: bodily actions, verbal actions, and mental actions. Since our bodily and verbal actions are initiated by our mental actions, ultimately the six realms are created by our mind. For example, a hell realm is a place that arises as a result of the worst actions, such as murder or extreme mental or physical cruelty, which depend upon the most deluded states of mind.

To form a mental image of the six realms, we can compare them to the floors of a large, old house. In this analogy, the house represents samsara, the cycle of contaminated rebirth that ordinary beings undergo without choice or control. The house has three storeys above ground and three below. Deluded sentient beings are like the inhabitants of this house. They are continually moving up and down the house, sometimes living above ground, sometimes below.

The ground floor corresponds to the human realm. Above this, on the first floor, is the realm of the demi-gods – non-human beings who are continually at war with the gods. In terms of power and prosperity, they are superior to human beings, but they are so obsessed with jealousy and violence that their lives have little spiritual value.

On the top floor live the gods. The lower classes of gods, the desire realm gods, live a life of ease and luxury, devoting their time to enjoyment and the satisfaction of their desires. Though their world is a paradise and their lifespan is very long, they are not immortal and they eventually fall to lower states. Since their lives are filled with distractions, it is difficult for them to find the motivation to practise Dharma, Buddha's teachings. From a spiritual point of view, a human life is much more meaningful than a god's life.

Higher than the desire realm gods are the gods of the form and formless realms. Having passed beyond sensual desire, the form realm gods experience the refined bliss of meditative absorption and possess bodies made of light. Transcending even these subtle forms, the gods of the formless realm abide without form in a subtle consciousness that resembles infinite space. Though their minds are the purest and most exalted within samsara, they have not overcome the ignorance of self-grasping, which is the root of samsara, and so, after experiencing bliss for many aeons, eventually their lives end and they are once again reborn in the lower states of samsara. Like the other gods, they consume the merit, or good fortune, they have created in the past and make little or no spiritual progress.

The three storeys above ground are called the "fortunate realms" because the beings who inhabit them have relatively pleasant experiences, which are caused by the practice of virtue. Below ground are the three lower realms, which are the result of negative bodily, verbal, and mental actions. The least painful of these is the animal realm, which, in the analogy, is the first floor beneath the ground. Included in this realm are all mammals apart from human beings, as well as birds, fish, insects, worms – the whole animal kingdom. Their minds are characterized by extreme stupidity, without any spiritual awareness, and their lives by fear and brutality.

On the next floor down live the hungry ghosts, or hungry spirits. The principal causes of rebirth here are greed and negative actions motivated by miserliness. The consequence of these actions is extreme poverty. Hungry spirits suffer hunger and thirst over a long period of time, which they find extremely difficult to bear. Their world is a vast desert. If by chance they come across a drop of water or a scrap of food, it disappears like a mirage or transforms into something repulsive, such as pus or urine. These appearances are due to their negative karma and lack of merit.

The lowest floor is hell. The beings here experience unrelenting torment. Some hells are a mass of fire, others are desolate regions of ice and darkness. Monsters conjured up by the minds of the hell beings inflict terrible tortures on them. The suffering continues unremittingly for what seems an eternity, but eventually the karma that caused the beings to be born in hell is exhausted and the hell beings die and are reborn elsewhere in samsara.

This is a general picture of samsara. We have been trapped in samsara since beginningless time, wandering meaninglessly, without any freedom or control, from the highest heaven to the deepest hell. Sometimes we dwell on the upper storeys as gods, and sometimes we find ourself on the ground floor with a human rebirth, but most of the time we are trapped on the underground floors, experiencing terrible physical and mental suffering.

Although samsara resembles a prison, there is however one door through which we can escape. That door is emptiness, the ultimate nature of phenomena. By training in the spiritual paths described in this book, we shall eventually find our way to this door and, stepping through, discover that the house was simply an illusion, the creation of our impure mind. Samsara is not an external prison; it is a prison made by our own mind. It will never end by itself but, by diligently practising the true spiritual path and thereby eliminating our self-grasping and other delusions, we can bring our samsara to an end. Once we attain liberation ourself, we shall then be in a position to show others how to destroy their mental prison by eradicating their delusions.

If we practise the twenty-one meditations presented in this book, we shall gradually overcome the deluded states of mind that keep us imprisoned in samsara and develop all the qualities needed to attain full enlightenment. The first six meditations function principally to help us to develop renunciation, the determination to escape from samsara. The next twelve meditations help us to cultivate heartfelt love and compassion for all living beings, and lead us to the realization that we can liberate others from samsara only by attaining enlightenment first. The principal obstacle that prevents us from attaining liberation and enlightenment is self-grasping, a deeply ingrained misconception of the way things exist. The main function of the next two meditations is to counter, and eventually to eradicate, this misconception. The final meditation is the method to gain deeper experience of the previous twenty meditations.

HOW TO MEDITATE

Each of the twenty-one meditation practices has five parts: preparation, contemplation, meditation, dedication, and subsequent practice. The instructions that explain these twenty-one meditation practices are called the "stages of the path", or "Lamrim". The realizations of these meditations are the actual spiritual paths that lead us to the great liberation of full enlightenment.

The first part, the preparatory practices, prepare us for successful meditation by purifying hindrances caused by our previous negative actions, by accumulating merit (or good fortune), and by enabling us to receive the blessings of enlightened beings. The preparatory practices are very important if we wish to gain deep experience of these meditations. For this purpose, we can begin our meditation with *Prayers for Meditation*, which can be found in Appendix I. A commentary to these practices can be found in Appendix II.

The purpose of the second part, contemplation, or analytical meditation, is to bring to mind the object of placement meditation. We do this by considering various lines of reasoning, contemplating analogies, and reflecting on the meaning of the instructions. It is helpful to memorize the contemplations given in each section so that we can meditate without having to look at the text. The contemplations given here are intended only as guidelines. We should supplement and enrich them with whatever reasons and examples we find helpful.

When, through our contemplations, the object appears clearly, we leave our analytical meditation and concentrate on the object single-pointedly. This single-pointed concentration is the third part, the actual meditation.

When we first start to meditate, our concentration is poor; we are easily distracted and often lose our object of meditation. Therefore, to begin with, we shall probably need to alternate between contemplation and placement meditation many times in each session. For example, if we are meditating on compassion, we begin by contemplating the various sufferings experienced by living beings until a strong feeling of compassion arises in our heart. When this feeling arises, we meditate on it single-pointedly. If the feeling fades, or if our mind wanders to another object, we should return to analytical meditation to bring the feeling back to mind. When the feeling of compassion has been restored, we once again leave our analytical meditation and hold the feeling with single-pointed concentration.

Both contemplation and meditation serve to acquaint our mind with virtuous objects. The more familiar we are with such objects, the more peaceful our mind becomes. By training in meditation, and living in accordance with the insights and resolutions developed during meditation, eventually we shall be able to maintain a peaceful mind continuously, throughout our life. More detailed instructions on the contemplations and on meditation in general can be found in *Transform Your Life* and *Joyful Path of Good Fortune*.

At the end of each session, we dedicate the merit produced by our meditation towards the attainment of enlightenment. If merit is not dedicated, it can easily be destroyed by anger. By reciting the dedication prayers sincerely at the end of each meditation session, we ensure that the merit we created by meditating is not wasted but acts as a cause of enlightenment.

The fifth part of each meditation practice is the subsequent practice. This consists of advice on how to integrate the meditation into our daily life. It is important to remember that Dharma practice is not confined to our activities during the meditation session; it should permeate our whole life. We should not allow a gulf to develop between our meditation and our daily life, because the success of our meditation depends upon the purity of our conduct outside the meditation session. We should keep a watch over our mind at all times by applying mindfulness, alertness, and conscientiousness; and we should try to abandon whatever bad habits we may have. Deep experience of Dharma is the result of practical training over a long period of time, both in and out of meditation. Therefore, we should practise steadily and gently, without being in a hurry to see results.

To summarize, our mind is like a field. Engaging in the preparatory practices is like preparing the field by removing obstacles caused by past negative actions, making it fertile with merit, and watering it with the blessings of the holy beings. Contemplation and meditation are like sowing good seeds, and dedication and subsequent practice are the methods for ripening our harvest of Dharma realizations.

Lamrim instructions are not given merely for the sake of intellectual understanding of the path to enlightenment. They are given to help us to gain deep experience, and should therefore be put into practice. If we train our mind in these meditations every day, eventually we shall gain perfect realizations of all the stages of the path. Until we have reached this stage, we should not tire of listening to oral teachings on Lamrim or reading authentic Lamrim commentaries, and then contemplating and meditating on these instructions. We need continually to expand our understanding of these essential topics and to use this new understanding to enhance our regular meditation.

If we genuinely wish to gain experience of the stages of the path, we should try to meditate every day. On the first day we can meditate on our precious human life, on the second day we can meditate on death and impermanence, and so on, until we complete the whole cycle in twenty-one days. Then we can begin again. Between sessions, we should try to remain mindful of the instructions on subsequent practice. Occasionally, when we have the opportunity, we should do a retreat on Lamrim. A suggested retreat schedule is given in Appendix IV. By practising like this, we use our whole life to further our experience of the stages of the path.

PART TWO

The Twenty-one Meditations

The Initial, Intermediate, and Great Scopes

In *Lamp for the Path to Enlightenment*, Atisha says, "You should know there are three types of living being: small, middling, and great." "Small", "middling", and "great" does not refer to their physical appearance, but to their different mental capacity or scope – initial, intermediate, and great. There are two types of small being: ordinary small beings and special small beings. Ordinary small beings are those who seek the happiness of only this life, and special small beings are those who seek the happiness of future lives. Middling beings are those who seek the happiness of liberation, and great beings are those who seek the happiness of enlightenment. Although there are countless living beings, all of them are included within these four types.

We should know which type of being we are now – an ordinary or special small being, a middling being, or a great being. Through the practice of Lamrim instructions, we can progress from the level of an ordinary small being to that of a special small being, and then a middling being, a great being, and finally an enlightened being. The practice of the following twenty-one meditations is the actual method for making this progress.

Through practising these meditations, we shall gain the realizations of all the stages of the path to enlightenment. The realizations of the first five meditations are the stages of the path of a person of initial scope; the realizations of the sixth meditation and the three higher trainings are the stages of the path of a person of intermediate scope; the realizations of the next fourteen meditations are the stages of the path of a person of great scope; and the realization of the last meditation can be a stage of the path of a person of initial, intermediate, or great scope.

The Initial Scope

1. OUR PRECIOUS HUMAN LIFE

The purpose of this meditation is to encourage ourself to practise Dharma. Dharma instructions teach us how to make ourself and others happy, how to control our delusions – especially our self-grasping, the root of all sufferings – and how to begin, make progress on, and complete the path to enlightenment, and are therefore important for everyone. If we put these teachings into practice, we can permanently cure the inner sickness of our delusions and all suffering, and achieve everlasting happiness. Therefore, we need to encourage ourself to practise Dharma and not waste our human life in meaningless activities. If we do not encourage ourself, no one will do this for us.

MEDITATION

As the preparatory practice, we recite *Prayers for Meditation* while concentrating on the meaning. Then we engage in the following contemplation:

> *Our human life is precious, rare, and immensely meaningful. Due to their previous deluded views that denied the value of spiritual practice, those who have taken rebirth as animals, for example, now have no opportunity to understand or practise Dharma. Since it is impossible for them to listen to, contemplate, and meditate on Dharma, their present animal rebirth itself is an obstacle. Only human beings are free from such obstacles and have all the necessary conditions for engaging in spiritual paths, which alone lead to everlasting happiness. This combination of freedom and*

possession of necessary conditions is the special characteristic that makes our human life so precious.

Although there are many human beings in this world, each one of us has only one life. One person may own many cars and houses, but even the richest person in the world cannot possess more than one life; and, when that is drawing to an end, he or she cannot buy, borrow, or manufacture another. When we lose this life, it will be very difficult to find another similarly qualified human life in the future. Therefore, for each of us, a human life is very rare.

If we use our human life to accomplish spiritual realizations, it becomes immensely meaningful. By using it in this way, we actualize our full potential and progress from the state of an ordinary, ignorant being to that of a fully enlightened being, the highest of all beings; and, when we have done this, we shall have the power to benefit all living beings without exception. Thus, by using our human life for gaining spiritual realizations, we can solve all our human problems and fulfil all our own and others' wishes. What could be more meaningful than this?

Having repeatedly contemplated these points, we make the strong determination: "I must practise Dharma." This determination is the object of our meditation. We then hold this without forgetting it; our mind should remain on this determination single-pointedly for as long as possible. If we lose the object of our meditation, we renew it by immediately remembering our determination or by repeating the contemplation.

At the end of the meditation session, we dedicate the virtues accumulated from this meditation practice towards the realization of the preciousness of our human life and the attainment of enlightenment for the happiness of all living beings.

During the meditation break, we try never to forget our determination to practise Dharma. We should apply strong effort to read Lamrim instructions and memorize their essential points, to recite prayers with strong faith, and to listen to oral teachings again and again and contemplate their meaning. Especially, we should put all the instructions into practice and integrate them into our daily life.

2. DEATH AND IMPERMANENCE

The purpose of this meditation is to eliminate the laziness of attachment, the main obstacle to practising Dharma purely. Because our desire for worldly enjoyment is so strong, we have little or no interest in spiritual practice. From a spiritual point of view, this lack of interest in spiritual practice is a type of laziness called the "laziness of attachment". For as long as we have this laziness, the door to liberation will be closed to us, and consequently we shall continue to experience misery in this life and endless suffering in life after life. The way to overcome this laziness is to meditate on death.

We need to contemplate and meditate on our death again and again until we gain a deep realization of death. Although on an intellectual level we all know that eventually we are going to die, our awareness of death remains superficial. Since our intellectual knowledge of death does not touch our hearts, each and every day we continue to think, "I shall not die today, I shall not die today." Even on the day of our death, we are still thinking about what we shall do tomorrow or next week. This mind that thinks every day, "I shall not die today", is deceptive – it leads us in the wrong direction and causes our human life to become empty. On the other hand, through meditating on death we shall gradually replace the deceptive thought, "I shall not die today", with the non-deceptive thought, "I may die today." The mind that spontaneously thinks each and every day, "I may die today", is the realization of death. It is this

Death destroys everything

realization that directly eliminates our laziness of attachment and opens the door to the spiritual path.

In general, we may die today or we may not die today – we do not know. However, if we think each day, "I may not die today", this thought will deceive us because it comes from our ignorance; whereas if instead we think each day, "I may die today", this thought will not deceive us because it comes from our wisdom. This beneficial thought will prevent our laziness of attachment, and will encourage us to prepare for the welfare of our countless future lives or to put great effort into entering the path to liberation. In this way, we shall make our human life meaningful.

MEDITATION

As the preparatory practice, we recite *Prayers for Meditation* while concentrating on the meaning. Then we engage in the following contemplation:

> *I shall definitely die. There is no way to prevent my body from finally decaying. Day by day, moment by moment, my life is slipping away. I have no idea when I shall die; the time of death is completely uncertain. Many young people die before their parents, some die the moment they are born – there is no certainty in this world. Furthermore, there are so many causes of untimely death. The lives of many strong and healthy people are destroyed by accidents. There is no guarantee that I shall not die today.*

Having repeatedly contemplated these points, we mentally repeat over and over again, "I may die today, I may die today", and concentrate on the feeling it evokes. Eventually we shall come to a conclusion: "Since I shall soon have to depart from this world, there is no sense in my becoming attached to the things of this life. Instead, I will devote my whole life to the practice of Dharma." This determination is the object of our meditation. We then hold this without forgetting it; our mind should remain on this determination single-pointedly for as long as possible. If we lose the object of our meditation, we renew it by immediately remembering our determination or by repeating the contemplation.

At the end of the meditation session, we dedicate the virtues accumulated from this meditation practice towards our realization of death and the attainment of enlightenment for the happiness of all living beings.

During the meditation break, we try to practise Dharma without laziness. Realizing that worldly pleasures are deceptive, and that they distract us from using our life in a meaningful way, we should abandon attachment to them. In this way, we can eliminate the main obstacle to pure Dharma practice.

3. THE DANGER OF LOWER REBIRTH

The purpose of this meditation is to encourage us to seek protection from the dangers of lower rebirth. If we do not prepare for protection from lower rebirth now, while we have a human life with its freedoms and endowments, once we have taken any of the three lower rebirths it will be extremely difficult to obtain a precious human life again. It is said to be easier for human beings to attain enlightenment than it is for beings in the lower realms, such as animals, to attain a human rebirth. This meditation encourages us to abandon non-virtue, to practise virtue, and to go for refuge to the holy beings, which is the actual protection from taking lower rebirth. Creating non-virtue is the main cause of taking lower rebirth, whereas practising virtue and going for refuge to the holy beings are the main causes of taking higher rebirth.

MEDITATION

As the preparatory practice, we recite *Prayers for Meditation* while concentrating on the meaning. Then we engage in the following contemplation:

> *When the oil of an oil lamp is exhausted, the flame goes out because the flame is produced from the oil; but when our body dies, our consciousness is not extinguished, because consciousness is not produced from the body. When we die, our mind has to leave this present body, which is just a temporary abode, and find another body, rather like a bird leaving one nest to fly to another. Our mind has no freedom to*

remain and no choice about where to go. We are blown to the place of our next rebirth by the winds of our karma. If the karma that ripens at our death time is negative, we shall definitely take a lower rebirth. Heavy negative karma causes rebirth in hell, less negative karma causes rebirth as a hungry spirit, and the least negative karma causes rebirth as an animal.

It is very easy to commit heavy negative karma. For example, simply by swatting a mosquito out of anger we create the cause to be reborn in hell. Throughout this and all our countless previous lives, we have committed many heavy negative actions. Unless we have already purified these actions by practising sincere confession, their potentialities remain in our mental continuum, and any one of these negative potentialities could ripen when we die. Bearing this in mind, we should ask ourself: "If I die today, where shall I be tomorrow? It is quite possible that I shall find myself in the animal realm, among the hungry spirits, or in hell. If someone were to call me a stupid cow today, I would find it difficult to bear, but what shall I do if I actually become a cow, a pig, or a fish?"

Having repeatedly contemplated these points, and understood how beings in the lower realms, such as animals, experience suffering, we generate a strong fear of taking rebirth in the lower realms. This feeling of fear is the object of our meditation. We then hold this without forgetting it; our mind should remain on this feeling of fear single-pointedly for as long as possible. If we lose the object of our meditation, we renew the feeling of fear by immediately remembering it or by repeating the contemplation.

At the end of the meditation session, we dedicate the virtues accumulated from this meditation practice towards the realization of the danger of our taking lower rebirth and the attainment of enlightenment for the happiness of all living beings.

During the meditation break, we try never to forget our feeling of fear of taking rebirth in the lower realms. In general, fear is meaningless, but the fear generated through the above contemplation and meditation has immense meaning, as it arises from wisdom and not ignorance. This fear is the main cause of going for refuge, which is the actual protection from such dangers, and helps us to be mindful and conscientious in avoiding non-virtuous actions.

4. REFUGE PRACTICE

The purpose of this meditation is to enable us to attain permanent liberation from lower rebirth. At present we are human and free from lower rebirth, but this is only a temporary and not a permanent liberation from lower rebirth. Until we gain a deep realization of refuge, we shall have to take lower rebirth again and again in countless future lives. We attain permanent liberation from lower rebirth by sincerely relying upon the Three Jewels: Buddha – the source of all refuge, Dharma – the realization of Buddha's teachings, and Sangha – pure Dharma practitioners who help us with our spiritual practice. Dharma is like medicine that prevents the sufferings of the three lower realms, Buddha is the doctor who gives us this medicine, and the Sangha are the nurses who assist us. Understanding this, we go for refuge to Buddha, Dharma, and Sangha.

MEDITATION

As the preparatory practice, we recite *Prayers for Meditation* while concentrating on the meaning. Then we engage in the following contemplation:

> *Through receiving Buddha's blessings and help from the Sangha, I shall accomplish profound Dharma realizations. Through this, I shall attain permanent liberation from lower rebirth.*

Having repeatedly contemplated this valid reason for going for refuge, we make the strong determination: "I must rely upon Buddha, Dharma, and Sangha as my ultimate refuge." This determination is the object of our meditation. We then hold this without forgetting it; our mind should remain on this determination single-pointedly for as long as possible. If we lose the object of our meditation, we renew it by immediately remembering our determination or by repeating the contemplation.

At the end of the meditation session, we dedicate the virtues accumulated from this meditation practice towards our realization of refuge and the attainment of enlightenment for the happiness of all living beings.

During the meditation break, we should practise the twelve commitments of refuge, which are explained in detail in Appendix V. Keeping the refuge commitments helps us to strengthen our refuge practice so that it quickly bears fruit.

5. ACTIONS AND THEIR EFFECTS

The purpose of this meditation is to encourage us to purify non-virtues, and to accumulate virtues that cause us to take human rebirth possessing freedoms and endowments in our future lives. In this context, "freedom" means freedom from physical and mental obstacles as well as those that arise from lacking conditions necessary for studying and practising Dharma. "Endowments" refers to having all the conditions needed for studying and practising Dharma.

An action, whether of body, speech, or mind, is called "karma" in Sanskrit. Engaging in the correct actions necessary for the welfare of our future lives depends upon a correct understanding of actions and their effects. All our actions of body, speech, and mind are causes and all our experiences are their effects. The law of karma explains why each individual has a unique mental disposition, a unique physical appearance, and unique experiences. These are the various effects of the countless actions that each individual has performed in the past. We cannot find any two people who have created exactly the same history of actions throughout their past lives, and so we cannot find two people with identical states of mind, identical experiences, or identical physical appearances. Each person has a different individual karma, which means they have different karmic experiences resulting from their own past actions. Some people enjoy good health, while others are constantly ill. Some people are very beautiful, while others are very ugly. Some people have a happy disposition that is easily pleased, while others have a sour disposition and are rarely delighted by anything.

Some people easily understand the meaning of spiritual teachings, while others find them difficult and obscure.

It is because of our karma or actions that we are born in this impure, contaminated world and experience so many difficulties and problems. Our actions are impure because our mind is contaminated by the inner poison of self-grasping. This is the fundamental reason why we experience suffering. Suffering is created by our own actions or karma – it is not given to us as a punishment. We suffer because we performed many non-virtuous actions in our previous lives, such as killing, stealing, deceiving others, destroying others' happiness, and holding wrong views. The source of these non-virtuous actions is our own delusions, such as anger, attachment, and self-grasping ignorance.

Once we have purified our mind of self-grasping and all other delusions, all our actions will naturally be pure. As a result of our pure actions or pure karma, everything we experience will be pure. We shall abide in a pure world, with a pure body, enjoying pure enjoyments and surrounded by pure beings. There will no longer be the slightest trace of suffering, impurity, or problems. This is how to find true happiness from within our mind.

MEDITATION

As the preparatory practice, we recite *Prayers for Meditation* while concentrating on the meaning. Then we engage in the following contemplation:

If I purify all my non-virtues, there will be no basis for me to take lower rebirth. By accumulating virtue, I shall take a human rebirth possessing freedoms and endowments in future lives. Thus, I can make progress along the path to enlightenment continually, life after life.

Having repeatedly contemplated these points, we make the strong determination: "I must purify all my non-virtues by sincerely engaging in the practice of confession, and I must put great effort into accumulating virtue." This determination is the object of our meditation. We then hold this without forgetting it; our mind should remain on this determination single-pointedly for as long as possible. If we lose the object of our meditation, we renew it by immediately remembering our determination or by repeating the contemplation.

At the end of the meditation session, we dedicate the virtues accumulated from this meditation practice towards our realization of karma and the attainment of enlightenment for the happiness of all living beings.

During the meditation break, we should conscientiously avoid even small non-virtuous actions, apply great effort to purifying the non-virtuous actions we have already created, and practise the virtuous actions of moral discipline, giving, patience, effort, concentration, and wisdom. These virtuous actions are the main causes of attaining a future human life possessing freedoms and endowments. Buddha said that a human rebirth comes from the practice of moral discipline, wealth comes from giving, a beautiful body comes from patience, the fulfilment of spiritual wishes comes from making effort in our Dharma study and practice, inner peace comes from concentration, and liberation comes from wisdom.

The Intermediate Scope

Taking rebirth in a fortunate realm, such as the human realm, is only like taking a short holiday if afterwards we have to descend to lower realms and once again experience extreme suffering for an inconceivably long time.

We experience suffering because we are in samsara. If we think deeply about this, we shall realize that if we want real freedom and happiness we must abandon samsara. By practising the stages of the path of a person of intermediate scope, we shall abandon samsara and attain permanent inner peace, completely free from all sufferings, fears, and their causes. This is real liberation.

6. DEVELOPING RENUNCIATION FOR SAMSARA

The purpose of this meditation is to develop the realization of renunciation – the spontaneous wish to attain liberation from samsara, the cycle of contaminated rebirth. Renunciation is the gateway through which we enter the path to liberation, or nirvana – the permanent inner peace attained through completely abandoning the ignorance of self-grasping.

In itself, our human rebirth is a true suffering; it is precious and valuable only when we use it to train in spiritual paths. We experience various types of suffering because we have taken a rebirth that is contaminated by the inner poison of delusions. This experience has no beginning, because we have taken contaminated rebirths since beginningless time, and it will have no end until we attain the supreme inner peace of nirvana. If we contemplate and meditate on how we experience sufferings and difficulties throughout this life, and in life after life, we shall come to the strong conclusion that every single one of our sufferings and problems arises because we have taken contaminated rebirth. We shall then develop a strong wish to abandon the cycle of contaminated rebirth, samsara. This is the first step towards attaining the happiness of nirvana. From this point of view, contemplating and meditating on suffering has great meaning.

For as long as we remain in this cycle of contaminated rebirth, suffering and problems will never end; we shall have to experience them over and over again every time we take rebirth. Although we cannot remember our experience while we were in our mother's womb or during our very early childhood, the sufferings of human life began from the time of our conception. Everyone can observe that a newborn baby experiences anguish and pain. The first thing a baby does when it is born is scream. Rarely has a baby ever been born in complete serenity, with a peaceful, smiling expression on its face.

In the following contemplations, we think about the various sufferings experienced in the human realm, but we should bear in mind that the sufferings of other realms are generally far worse.

Birth

When our consciousness first enters the union of our father's sperm and our mother's ovum, our body is a hot, watery substance like white yoghurt tinted red. In the first moments after conception, we have no gross feelings but, as soon as these develop, we begin to experience pain. Our body gradually becomes harder and harder and, as our limbs grow, it feels as if our body is being stretched out on a rack. Inside our mother's womb it is hot and dark. Our home for nine months is this small, tightly compressed space full of unclean substances. It is like being squashed inside a small water tank full of filthy liquid with the lid tightly shut so that no air or light can come through.

While we are in our mother's womb, we experience much pain and fear all on our own. We are extremely sensitive to everything our mother does. When she walks quickly, it feels as if we are falling from a high mountain and we are terrified. If she has sexual intercourse, it feels as

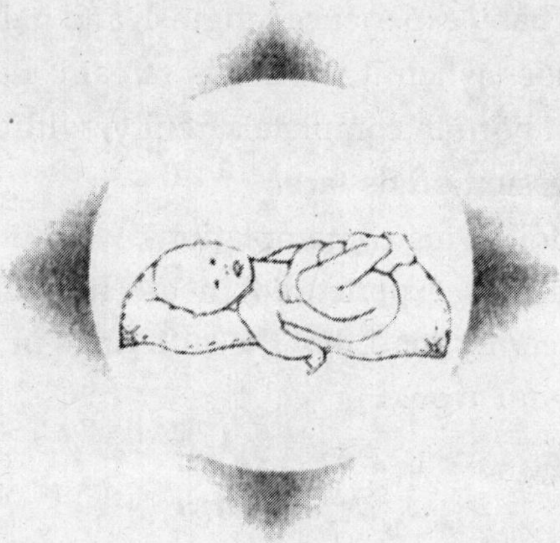

Birth brings all suffering

if we are being crushed and suffocated between two huge weights and we panic. If our mother makes just a small jump, it feels as if we are being dashed against the ground from a great height. If she drinks anything hot, it feels like boiling water scalding our skin, and if she drinks anything cold, it feels like an icy-cold shower in midwinter.

When we are emerging from our mother's womb, it feels as if we are being forced through a narrow crevice between two hard rocks, and when we are newly born our body is so delicate that any kind of contact is painful. Even if someone holds us very tenderly, his or her hands feel like thorn bushes piercing our flesh, and the most delicate fabrics feel rough and abrasive. By comparison with the softness and smoothness of our mother's womb, every tactile sensation is harsh and painful. If someone picks us up, it feels as if we are being swung over a huge precipice and we feel frightened and insecure. We have forgotten all that we knew in our previous life; we bring only pain and confusion from our mother's womb. Whatever we hear is as meaningless as the sound of wind and we cannot comprehend anything we perceive. In the first few weeks, we are like someone who is blind, deaf, and dumb, and suffering from profound amnesia. When we are hungry we cannot say, "I need food", and when we are in pain we cannot say, "This is hurting me." The only signs we can make are hot tears and furious gestures. Our mother often has no idea what pains and discomforts we are experiencing. We are completely helpless and have to be taught everything – how to eat, how to sit, how to walk, how to talk.

Although we are most vulnerable in the first few weeks of our life, our pains do not cease as we grow up. We continue to experience various kinds of suffering throughout our life. Just as when we light a fire in a large house, the heat from the fire pervades the whole house and all the heat in the house comes from the fire, so, when we are born in samsara, suffering pervades our whole life and all the miseries we experience arise because we took a contaminated rebirth.

Since we have been born as a human being, we cherish our human body and mind and cling to them as our own. In dependence upon observing our body and mind, we develop self-grasping, which is the root of all delusions. Our human rebirth is the basis of our human suffering; without this basis, there are no human problems. The pains of birth gradually turn into the pains of sickness, ageing, and death – they are one continuum.

Sickness

Our birth gives rise to the sufferings of sickness. Just as the wind and snow of winter take away the glory of green meadows, trees, forests, and flowers, so sickness takes away the youthful splendour of our body, destroying its strength and the power of our senses. If we are usually fit and well, when we become sick we are suddenly unable to engage in all our normal physical activities. Even a champion boxer who is usually able to knock out all his opponents becomes completely helpless when sickness strikes.

When we fall ill, we are like a bird that has been soaring in the sky and is suddenly shot down. When a bird is shot, all its glory and power are immediately destroyed and it falls straight to the ground like a lump of lead. In a similar way, when we become ill we are suddenly incapacitated. If we are seriously ill, we may become completely dependent upon others and lose the ability to control even our bodily functions. This transformation is hard to bear, especially for those who pride themselves on their independence and physical well-being.

When we are ill, we feel frustrated as we cannot do our usual work or complete all the tasks we have set ourself. We easily become impatient with our illness and depressed about all the things we cannot do. We cannot enjoy the things that usually give us pleasure, such as sport, dancing, drinking, eating rich foods, or the company of our friends. All these limitations make us feel even more miserable, and, to add to our unhappiness, we have to endure all the physical pains the illness brings.

When we are sick, not only do we have to experience all the unwanted pains of the illness itself, but we also have to experience all sorts of other unwished for things. For example, we have to take whatever cure is prescribed, whether it be a foul-tasting medicine, a series of injections, a major operation, or abstinence from something we like very much. If we are to have an operation, we have to go to hospital and accept all the conditions there. We may have to eat food we do not like and stay in bed all day long with nothing to do, and we may feel anxiety about the operation. Our doctor may not explain to us exactly what the problem is and whether or not he or she expects us to survive.

If we learn that our sickness is incurable, and we have no spiritual experience, we shall suffer anxiety, fear, and regret. We may become depressed and give up hope, or we may become angry with our illness, feeling that it is an enemy that has maliciously deprived us of all joy.

Ageing

Our birth also gives rise to the pains of ageing. Ageing steals our beauty, our health, our good figure, our fine complexion, our vitality, and our comfort. Ageing turns us into objects of contempt. It brings many unwanted pains and takes us swiftly to our death.

As we grow old, we lose all the beauty of our youth, and our strong, healthy body becomes weak and burdened with illness. Our once firm and well-proportioned figure becomes bent and disfigured, and our muscles and flesh shrink so that our limbs become like thin sticks and our bones poke out. Our hair loses its colour and shine and our complexion loses its lustre. Our face becomes wrinkled and our features grow distorted. Milarepa said:

> How do old people get up? They get up as if they were heaving a stake out of the ground. How do old people walk about? Once they are on their feet, they have to walk gingerly, like bird-catchers. How do old people sit down? They crash down like heavy luggage whose harness has snapped.

We can contemplate the following poem on the sufferings of growing old:

When we are old, our hair becomes white,
But not because we have washed it clean;
It is a sign we shall soon encounter the Lord of
  Death.

We have wrinkles on our forehead,
But not because we have too much flesh;
It is a warning from the Lord of Death: "You are
  about to die."

Our teeth fall out,
But not to make room for new ones;
It is a sign we shall soon lose the ability to eat
  human food.

Our faces are ugly and unpleasant,
But not because we are wearing masks;
It is a sign we have lost the mask of youth.

Our heads shake to and fro,
But not because we are in disagreement;
It is the Lord of Death striking our head with the
  stick he holds in his right hand.

We walk bent and gazing at the ground,
But not because we are searching for lost needles;
It is a sign we are searching for our lost beauty and
  memories.

We get up from the ground using all four limbs,
But not because we are imitating animals;
It is a sign our legs are too weak to support our
bodies.

We sit down as if we had suddenly fallen,
But not because we are angry;
It is a sign our body has lost its strength.

Our body sways as we walk,
But not because we think we are important;
It is a sign our legs cannot carry our body.

Our hands shake,
But not because they are itching to steal;
It is a sign the Lord of Death's itchy fingers are
stealing our possessions.

We eat very little,
But not because we are miserly;
It is a sign we cannot digest our food.

We wheeze frequently,
But not because we are whispering mantras to the
sick;
It is a sign our breathing will soon disappear.

When we are young, we can travel around the whole world, but when we are old we can hardly make it to our own front gate. We become too weak to engage in many worldly activities, and our spiritual activities are often curtailed. For example, we have little physical strength to perform virtuous actions, and mentally we have less energy to memorize, contemplate, and meditate. We cannot attend teachings that are given in places that are hard to reach or uncomfortable to inhabit. We cannot help others in ways that require physical strength and good health. Deprivations such as these often make old people very sad.

When we grow old, we become like someone who is blind and deaf. We cannot see clearly, and we need stronger and stronger glasses until we can no longer read. We cannot hear clearly, and so it becomes more and more difficult to listen to music or to the television or to hear what others are saying. Our memory fades. All activities, worldly and spiritual, become more difficult. If we practise meditation, it becomes harder for us to gain realizations, because our memory and concentration are too weak. We cannot apply ourself to study. Thus, if we have not learnt and trained in spiritual practices when we were younger, the only thing to do when we grow old is to develop regret and wait for the Lord of Death to come.

When we are old, we cannot derive the same enjoyment from the things we used to enjoy, such as food, drink, and sex. We are too weak to play games and we are often too exhausted even for entertainments. As our lifespan runs out, we cannot join young people in their activities. When they travel about, we have to stay behind. No one wants to take us with them when we are old and no one wants to visit us. Even our own grandchildren do not want to stay with us for very long. Old people often think to themselves, "How wonderful it would be if young people would stay with me. We could go out for walks and I could show them things"; but young people do not want to be included in their plans. As their life draws to an end, old people experience the sorrow of abandonment and loneliness. They have many special sorrows.

Death

Our birth also gives rise to the sufferings of death. If during our life we have worked hard to acquire possessions, and if we have become very attached to them, we shall experience great suffering at the time of death, thinking, "Now I have to leave all my precious possessions behind." Even now, we find it difficult to lend one of our most treasured possessions to someone else, let alone to give it away. No wonder we become so miserable when we realize that, in the hands of death, we must abandon everything.

When we die, we have to part from even our closest friends. We have to leave our partner, even though we may have been together for years and never spent a day apart. If we are very attached to our friends, we shall experience great misery at the time of death, but all we shall be able to do is hold their hands. We shall not be able to halt the process of death, even if they plead with us not to die. Usually, when we are very attached to someone, we feel jealous if he or she leaves us on our own and spends time with someone else, but when we die we shall have to leave our friends with others forever. We shall have to leave everyone, including our family and all the people who have helped us in this life.

When we die, this body that we have cherished and cared for in so many ways will have to be left behind. It will become mindless like a stone and will be buried in the ground or cremated. If we do not have the inner protection of spiritual experience, at the time of death we shall experience fear and distress, as well as physical pain.

When our consciousness departs from our body at death, all the potentialities we have accumulated in our mind by performing virtuous and non-virtuous actions will go with it. Other than these, we cannot take anything else out of this world. All other things deceive us. Death ends all our activities – our conversation, our eating, our meeting with friends, our sleep. Everything draws to a close on the day of our death and we must leave all things behind, even the rings on our fingers. In Tibet, beggars carry a stick to defend themselves against dogs. To understand the complete deprivation of death, we should remember that at the time of death beggars have to leave even this old stick, the most meagre of human possessions. All over the world, we can see that names carved on stone are the only possessions of the dead.

Other types of suffering

We also have to experience the sufferings of separation, having to encounter what we do not like, and failing to satisfy our desires. Before the final separation at the time of death, we often have to experience temporary separation from the people and things we like, which causes us mental pain. We may have to leave our country where all our friends and relatives live, or we may have to leave the job we like. We may lose our reputation. Many times in this life we have to experience the misery of departing from the people we like, or forsaking and losing the things we find pleasant and attractive, but when we die we have to part forever from all the companions and enjoyments of this life.

We often have to meet and live with people whom we do not like or encounter situations that we find unpleasant. Sometimes we may find ourself in a very dangerous situation such as in a fire or a flood, or where there is violence such as in a riot or a battle. Our lives are full of less extreme situations that we find annoying. Sometimes we are prevented from doing the things we want to do. On a sunny day, we may set off for the beach but find ourself stuck in a traffic jam. We continually experience interference from our inner demon of delusions, which disturbs our mind and our spiritual practices. There are countless conditions that frustrate our plans and prevent us from doing what we want. It is as if we are naked and living in a thorn bush – whenever we try to move, we are wounded by circumstances. People and things are like thorns piercing our flesh and no situation ever feels entirely comfortable. The more desires and plans we have, the more frustrations we experience. The more we want certain situations, the more we find ourself stuck in situations we do not want. Every desire seems to invite its own obstacle. Undesired situations befall us without our looking for them. In fact, the only things that come effortlessly are the things we do not want. No one wants to die, but death comes effortlessly. No one wants to be sick, but sickness comes effortlessly. Since we have taken rebirth without freedom or control, we have an impure body and inhabit an impure environment, and so undesirable things pour in upon us. In samsara, this kind of experience is entirely natural.

We have countless desires but, no matter how much effort we make, we never feel that we have satisfied them. Even when we get what we want, we do not get it in the way we want. We possess the object but we do not derive satisfaction from possessing it. For example, we may dream of becoming wealthy, but, if we actually become wealthy, our life is not the way we imagined it would be and we do not feel that we have fulfilled our desire. This is because our desires do not decrease as our wealth increases. The more wealth we have, the more we desire. The wealth we seek is unfindable because we seek an amount that will satiate our desires and no amount of wealth can do that. To make things worse, in obtaining the object of our desire we create new occasions for discontent. With every object we desire come other objects we do not want. For example, with wealth come taxes, insecurity, and complicated financial affairs. These unwished for accessories prevent us from ever feeling fully satisfied. Similarly, we may dream of having a holiday in the South Seas, and we may actually go there on holiday, but the experience is never quite what we expect, and with our holiday come other things such as sunburn and great expense.

If we examine our desires, we shall see that they are inordinate. We want all the best things in samsara – the best job, the best partner, the best reputation, the best house, the best car, the best holiday. Anything that is not the best leaves us with a feeling of disappointment – still searching for but not finding what we want. No worldly enjoyment, however,

In this cycle of samsara

there is no real happiness

can give us the complete and perfect satisfaction we desire. Better things are always being produced. Everywhere, new advertisements announce that the very best thing has just arrived on the market, but a few days later another best thing arrives that is better than the best thing of a few days ago. There is no end of new things to captivate our desires.

Children at school can never satisfy their own or their parents' ambitions. Even if they come top of their class, they feel they cannot be content unless they do the same the following year. If they go on to be successful in their jobs, their ambitions will be as strong as ever. There is no point at which they can rest, feeling that they are completely satisfied with what they have done.

We may think that at least people who lead a simple life in the country must be content, but, if we look at their situation, we shall find that even farmers search for but do not find what they want. Their lives are full of problems and anxieties and they do not enjoy real peace and satisfaction. Their livelihoods depend upon many uncertain factors beyond their control, such as the weather. Farmers have no more freedom from discontent than businessmen who live and work in the city. Businessmen look smart and efficient as they set off to work each morning carrying their briefcases but, although they look so smooth on the outside, in their hearts they carry many dissatisfactions. They are still searching for but not finding what they want.

If we reflect on this situation, we may decide that we can find what we are searching for by abandoning all our possessions. We can see, however, that even poor people are looking for but not finding what they seek, and many poor people have difficulty in finding even the most basic necessities of life.

We cannot avoid the suffering of dissatisfaction by frequently changing our situation. We may think that if we keep getting a new partner or a new job, or keep travelling about, we shall eventually find what we want; but even if we were to travel to every place on the globe, and have a new lover in every town, we would still be seeking another place and another lover. In samsara, there is no real fulfilment of our desires.

Whenever we see anyone in a high or low position, male or female, they differ only in appearance, dress, behaviour, and status. In essence they are all equal – they all experience problems in their lives. Whenever we have a problem, it is easy to think that it is caused by our particular circumstances and that, if we were to change our circumstances, our problem would disappear. We blame other people, our friends, our food, our government, our times, the weather, society, history, and so forth. However, external circumstances such as these are not the main causes of our problems. We need to recognize that these painful experiences are the consequences of our taking a rebirth that is contaminated by the inner poison of delusions. Human beings have to experience human sufferings because they took a contaminated human rebirth. Animals have to experience animal suffering, and hungry spirits and hell beings similarly have to experience their own particular sufferings because they took a contaminated rebirth. Even gods are not free from suffering, because they too have taken a contaminated rebirth.

MEDITATION

As the preparatory practice, we recite *Prayers for Meditation* while concentrating on the meaning. Then we engage in the following contemplation:

> *Unless I attain liberation from samsara – the cycle of contaminated rebirth – I shall have to experience again and again, in life after life, endlessly, the sufferings of birth, sickness, ageing, death, having to part with what I like, having to encounter what I do not like, and failing to satisfy my desires.*

Having repeatedly contemplated this point, we make the strong determination: "I must abandon samsara and attain the supreme inner peace of liberation." This determination is the object of our meditation. We then hold this without forgetting it; our mind should remain on this determination single-pointedly for as long as possible. If we lose the object of our meditation, we renew it by immediately remembering our determination or by repeating the contemplation.

At the end of the meditation session, we dedicate the virtues accumulated from this meditation practice towards our realization of renunciation and the attainment of enlightenment for the happiness of all living beings.

During the meditation break, we try never to forget our determination to abandon samsara and attain liberation. When we meet with difficult circumstances, or see others experiencing difficulties, we should use these to remind ourself of the disadvantages of samsara. When things are going well, we should not be deceived, but recall that samsaric pleasures are short-lived and deceptive. In this way, we can use all our experiences of daily life to strengthen our practice of renunciation.

The actual method to abandon samsara and to attain liberation is the practice of the three higher trainings – the trainings in moral discipline, concentration, and wisdom, motivated by renunciation. Using the body of moral discipline, the hand of concentration, and the axe of wisdom realizing emptiness, we can cut the poisonous tree of our self-grasping and thus destroy all its branches, our other delusions. Through this, we shall experience permanent inner peace – actual liberation, nirvana.

Come under the Mahayana umbrella

The Great Scope

We should maintain renunciation – the wish to abandon samsara and attain liberation – day and night. It is the main path to liberation and the basis of more advanced realizations. However, we should not be content with seeking merely our own liberation; we need also to consider the welfare of other living beings. There are countless beings trapped in the prison of samsara experiencing an unlimited variety of sufferings. Whereas each one of us is just one single person, other people are countless in number; therefore, the happiness of others is much more important than our own happiness. For this reason, we must enter the Mahayana path, the supreme method for benefiting all living beings. Mahayana means the "great vehicle to enlightenment". The gateway through which we enter the Mahayana path is by generating the mind that spontaneously wishes to attain enlightenment for the benefit of all living beings. This precious mind is called "bodhichitta".

7. DEVELOPING EQUANIMITY

The purpose of this meditation is to free our mind from unbalanced attitudes, which are the main obstacle to developing the essential Mahayana realizations of unbiased love, compassion, and bodhichitta. Our feelings towards others are normally unbalanced. When we see a friend or someone we find particularly attractive, we feel pleased; when we see an enemy or an unattractive person, we feel dislike for him or her; and when we see a stranger or someone we find neither attractive nor unattractive, we feel indifference. For as long as we have these unbalanced attitudes, our mind will be like a rocky field that cannot support the growth of Mahayana realizations. Our first task, therefore, is to free our mind from these unbalanced attitudes and develop genuine equanimity – an equally warm and friendly attitude towards all living beings.

MEDITATION

As the preparatory practice, we recite *Prayers for Meditation* while concentrating on the meaning. Then we engage in the following contemplation:

There is no sense in feeling attached to someone who appears attractive, feeling aversion towards someone who appears unattractive, or feeling indifferent towards someone who is neither attractive nor unattractive. Someone who appears attractive to me can be an object of aversion to others; someone who appears unattractive to me can be an object of attachment to others; and someone to whom I feel indifferent can be an object of attachment or aversion to others. There is no certainty. The appearances of attractiveness, unattractiveness, and indifference are only my own mistaken projections; and they make my mind unbalanced and unpeaceful, and destroy my happiness.

Having repeatedly contemplated these points, we make the strong determination: "I must stop these unbalanced minds, and develop and maintain equanimity – an equally warm and friendly attitude towards all living beings." With this determination, we generate a warm and friendly feeling towards all living beings without exception. This feeling of equanimity is the object of our meditation. We then hold this without forgetting it; our mind should remain on this feeling of equanimity single-pointedly for as long as possible. If we lose the object of our meditation, we renew it by immediately remembering our determination or by repeating the contemplation.

At the end of the meditation session, we dedicate the virtues accumulated from this meditation practice towards our realization of equanimity and the attainment of enlightenment for the happiness of all living beings.

During the meditation break, we maintain this feeling of equanimity day and night, keeping in our heart a warm feeling towards everyone we meet or think about. If we do this, there will be no basis for the problems of attachment or anger to arise, and our mind will remain at peace all the time.

Always live

in harmony and peace

8. RECOGNIZING THAT ALL LIVING BEINGS ARE OUR MOTHERS

Generating bodhichitta, the main path to enlightenment, depends upon universal compassion and cherishing love, which in turn depend upon affectionate love. To enhance our affectionate love for all living beings, we begin by contemplating how they are all our mothers.

Since it is impossible to find a beginning to our mental continuum, it follows that we have taken countless rebirths in the past, and, if we have had countless rebirths, we must have had countless mothers. Where are all these mothers now? They are all the living beings alive today.

It is incorrect to reason that our mothers of former lives are no longer our mothers just because a long time has passed since they actually cared for us. If our present mother were to die today, would she cease to be our mother? No, we would still regard her as our mother and pray for her happiness. The same is true of all our previous mothers – they died, yet they remain our mothers. It is only because of the changes in our external appearance that we do not recognize each other.

In our daily life, we see many different living beings, both human and non-human. We regard some as friends, some as enemies, and most as strangers. These distinctions are made by our mistaken minds; they are not verified by valid minds. Rather than following such mistaken minds, it would be better to regard all living beings as our mothers. Whoever we meet, we should think, "This person is my mother." In this way, we shall feel equally warm towards all living beings.

If we regard all living beings as our mothers, we shall find it easy to develop pure love and compassion, our everyday relationships will become pure and stable, and we shall naturally avoid negative actions such as killing or harming living beings. Since it is so beneficial to regard all living beings as our mothers, we should adopt this way of thinking without hesitation.

MEDITATION

As the preparatory practice, we recite *Prayers for Meditation* while concentrating on the meaning. Then we engage in the following contemplation:

> *Since it is impossible to find a beginning to my mental continuum, it follows that I have taken countless rebirths in the past, and, if I have had countless rebirths, I must have had countless mothers. Where are all these mothers now? They are all the living beings alive today.*

Having repeatedly contemplated this point, we generate a strong recognition that all living beings are our mothers. This recognition is the object of our meditation. We then hold this without forgetting it; our mind should remain on this recognition single-pointedly for as long as possible. If we lose the object of our meditation, we renew it by immediately remembering our recognition or by repeating the contemplation.

At the end of the meditation session, we dedicate the virtues accumulated from this meditation practice towards the realization that all living beings are our mothers and the attainment of enlightenment for the happiness of all living beings.

During the meditation break, we maintain this recognition day and night. We should regard everyone we meet as our mother. This applies even to animals and insects, as well as to our enemies. Instead of discriminating people as friends, enemies, or strangers, we should try to view them all equally as being our mother. In this way, we shall overcome the harmful attitudes of attachment, hatred, and indifference.

Practise the teachings of

the Wheel of Dharma

9. REMEMBERING THE KINDNESS OF LIVING BEINGS

Having become convinced that all living beings are our mothers, we contemplate the immense kindness we have received from each of them when they were our mother, as well as the kindness they have shown us at other times.

When we were conceived, had our mother not wanted to keep us in her womb she could have had an abortion. If she had done so, we would not now have this human life. Through her kindness she allowed us to stay in her womb, and so we now enjoy a human life and experience all its advantages. When we were a baby, had we not received her constant care and attention we would certainly have had an accident and could now be handicapped, crippled, or blind. Fortunately, our mother did not neglect us. Day and night, she gave us her loving care, regarding us as more important than herself. She saved our life many times each day. During the night she allowed her sleep to be interrupted, and during the day she forfeited her usual pleasures. She had to leave her job, and when her friends went out to enjoy themselves she had to stay behind. She spent all her money on us, giving us the best food and the best clothes she could afford. She taught us how to eat, how to walk, how to talk. Thinking of our future welfare, she did her best to ensure that we received a good education. Due to her kindness, we are now able to study whatever we choose. It is principally through the kindness of our mother that we now have the opportunity to practise Dharma and eventually to attain enlightenment.

Since there is no one who has not been our mother at some time in our previous lives, and since when we were their child they treated us with the same kindness as our present mother has treated us in this life, all living beings are very kind.

The kindness of living beings is not limited to the times when they have been our mother. All the time, our day-to-day needs are provided through the kindness of others. We brought nothing with us from our former life, yet, as soon as we were born, we were given a home, food, clothes, and everything we needed – all provided through the kindness of others. Everything we now enjoy has been provided through the kindness of other beings, past or present.

We are able to make use of many things with very little effort on our own part. If we consider facilities such as roads, cars, trains, aeroplanes, ships, houses, restaurants, hotels, libraries, hospitals, shops, money, and so on, it is clear that many people worked very hard to provide these things. Even though we make little or no contribution towards the provision of these facilities, they are all available for us to use. This shows the great kindness of others.

Both our general education and our spiritual training are provided by others. All our Dharma realizations, from our very first insights up to our eventual attainment of liberation and enlightenment, will be attained in dependence upon the kindness of others.

MEDITATION

As the preparatory practice, we recite *Prayers for Meditation* while concentrating on the meaning. Then, focusing on all living beings, we engage in the following contemplation:

In previous lives, when I was their child, they treated me with the same kindness as my present mother has treated me in this life.

The kindness of these living beings is not limited to the times when they have been my mother; all the time, my day-to-day needs are provided through their kindness. My general education, my spiritual training, and all my Dharma realizations – from my very first insights up to my eventual attainment of liberation and enlightenment – are attained in dependence upon the kindness of these living beings.

Having repeatedly contemplated the kindness of all living beings, we generate a strong feeling of affectionate love for them. This feeling is the object of our meditation. We then hold this without forgetting it; our mind should remain on this feeling of affectionate love for all living beings single-pointedly for as long as possible. If we lose the object of our meditation, we renew it by immediately remembering our feeling of affectionate love or by repeating the contemplation.

At the end of the meditation session, we dedicate the virtues accumulated from this meditation practice towards our realization of affectionate love for all living beings and the attainment of enlightenment for their happiness.

During the meditation break, throughout all our activities we maintain the feeling of affectionate love for every living being we meet or think about. Maintaining this special feeling will prevent us from harming others out of anger or attachment.

10. EQUALIZING SELF AND OTHERS

To equalize self and others is to cherish others as much as we cherish ourself. Until now, we have cherished only ourself. The purpose of this meditation is to share our feeling of cherishing so that we come to cherish ourself and all living beings equally.

MEDITATION

As the preparatory practice, we recite *Prayers for Meditation* while concentrating on the meaning. Then we engage in the following contemplation:

I will cherish myself and others equally because:

1. *All living beings have shown me great kindness in both this and previous lives.*
2. *Just as I wish to be free from suffering and experience only happiness, so do all other beings. In this respect, I am no different from any other being; we are all equal.*
3. *I am only one, whereas others are countless, so how can I cherish myself alone while I neglect to cherish others? My happiness and suffering are insignificant when compared with the happiness and suffering of all other living beings.*

Having repeatedly contemplated these points, we generate a feeling of cherishing all living beings equally. This feeling is the object of our meditation. We then hold this without forgetting it; our mind should remain on this feeling single-pointedly for as long as possible. If we lose the object of our meditation, we renew it by immediately remembering our feeling of cherishing all living beings equally or by repeating the contemplation.

At the end of the meditation session, we dedicate the virtues accumulated from this meditation practice towards our realization of equalizing self and others and the attainment of enlightenment for the happiness of all living beings.

During the meditation break, whenever we meet or think of any living being, we try to cherish them sincerely, always regarding their happiness and freedom as very important. If we train in this way, many of the problems we experience in daily life will disappear because most of our problems arise from regarding ourself as more important than others.

Enjoy the inner wealth of

faith and compassion

11. THE DISADVANTAGES OF SELF-CHERISHING

When we think "I" and "mine", we perceive an inherently existent I, and we cherish it and believe that its happiness and freedom are the most important. This is self-cherishing. Self-cherishing is our normal view that believes "I am important" and "My happiness and freedom are important", and that neglects others' happiness and freedom. It is part of our ignorance because in reality there is no inherently existent I. Our self-cherishing mind nevertheless cherishes this I and believes it to be the most important. It is a foolish and deceptive mind that always interferes with our inner peace, and it is a great obstacle to our accomplishing the real meaning of our human life.

We have had this self-cherishing mind in life after life since beginningless time, even while asleep and dreaming. To fulfil our selfish intentions, we previously committed many non-virtuous actions that caused others to experience suffering and problems. As a result of these actions, we now experience suffering and many problems.

In *Guide to the Bodhisattva's Way of Life*, Shantideva says:

> ... all the suffering there is in this world
> Arises from wishing ourself to be happy.

Sufferings are not given to us as a punishment. They all come from our self-cherishing mind, which wishes ourself to be happy while neglecting the happiness of others. There are two ways to understand this. First, the self-cherishing mind is the creator of all our suffering and problems; and second, self-cherishing is the basis for experiencing all our suffering and problems.

We suffer because we performed actions that caused others to experience suffering. These actions were created by selfish intentions – our self-cherishing. As a result of these actions, we now experience our present suffering and problems. Therefore, the real creator of all our suffering and problems is our self-cherishing mind.

Our present experience of particular suffering and problems has a special connection with particular actions we performed in our previous lives. This is very subtle. We cannot see this hidden connection with our eyes, but we can understand it through using our wisdom, and in particular through relying upon Buddha's teachings. In general, everyone knows that if they perform bad actions they will experience bad results and if they perform good actions they will experience good results.

The self-cherishing mind is also the basis for experiencing all our suffering and problems. For example, when people are unable to fulfil their wishes, many experience depression, discouragement, unhappiness, and mental pain, and some even want to kill themselves. This is because their self-cherishing believes that their own wishes are so important. It is therefore their self-cherishing that is mainly responsible for their unhappiness. Without self-cherishing, there would be no basis for experiencing such suffering and problems.

When we are ill, we find it difficult to accept our suffering, but illness harms us only because we cherish ourself. If another person is experiencing a similar illness, we have no problem. Why? Because we do not cherish him or her. However, if we cherished others as we cherish ourself, we would find it difficult to bear his suffering. This is compassion. As Shantideva says:

The suffering I experience
Does not harm others,
But I find it hard to bear
Because I cherish myself.

Likewise, the suffering of others
Does not harm me,
But, if I cherish others,
I shall find their suffering hard to bear.

In life after life, since beginningless time, we have tried to fulfil the wishes of our self-cherishing mind, believing its view to be true. We have put great effort into seeking happiness from external sources, but have nothing to show for it now. Because self-cherishing has deceived us, we have wasted countless previous lives. It has driven us to work for our own purpose, but we have gained nothing. This foolish mind has made all our previous lives empty – when we took this human rebirth, we brought nothing with us but delusions. In every moment of every day, this self-cherishing mind continues to deceive us.

MEDITATION

As the preparatory practice, we recite *Prayers for Meditation* while concentrating on the meaning. Then, remembering the many faults and disadvantages of self-cherishing as mentioned above, we think:

Nothing causes me greater harm than the demon of my self-cherishing. It is the source of all my negativity, misfortune, problems, and suffering.

Having repeatedly contemplated this point, we make the strong determination: "I must abandon my self-cherishing." This determination is the object of our meditation. We then hold this without forgetting it; our mind should remain on this determination single-pointedly for as long as possible. If we lose the object of our meditation, we renew it by immediately remembering our determination or by repeating the contemplation.

At the end of the meditation session, we dedicate the virtues accumulated from this meditation practice towards our realization of the disadvantages of self-cherishing and the attainment of enlightenment for the happiness of all living beings.

During the meditation break, we should be ever mindful of the faults of self-cherishing and, by repeatedly recalling the determination we made in meditation, try gradually to abandon it. Whenever we experience difficulties or suffering, we should not blame other people or the external situation – rather, we should remember that ultimately all our problems arise from self-cherishing. Therefore, when things go wrong, we should blame only our self-cherishing mind. By practising in this way, our self-cherishing, the root of all faults, will gradually diminish and eventually cease altogether.

12. THE ADVANTAGES OF CHERISHING OTHERS

When we think that others are important, and that their happiness and freedom are important, we are cherishing others. If we cherish others, we shall naturally perform actions that will cause them to be happy. This will make our daily life peaceful, happy, harmonious, and meaningful. We can begin this practice with our family, friends, and those who surround us, and then gradually extend this to all living beings without exception. In this way, we shall show the best example of pure Dharma practice.

In *Guide to the Bodhisattva's Way of Life*, Shantideva says:

All the happiness there is in this world
Arises from wishing others to be happy.

If we think carefully, we shall realize that all our present and future happiness depends upon our cherishing others – upon our wanting others to be happy. In our past lives, because we cherished others, we practised moral discipline, such as refraining from killing or harming others and abandoning stealing from them. Sometimes, out of fondness for them, we practised giving and patience. As a result of these positive actions, we have now obtained this precious human life. Moreover, because sometimes in the past we helped others and gave them protection, we ourself now receive help and enjoy pleasant conditions.

If we sincerely practise cherishing others, we shall experience many benefits in this and future lives. The immediate effect will be that many of our problems, such as those that arise from anger, jealousy, and selfish behaviour, will disappear, and our mind will become calm and peaceful. Since we shall act in considerate ways, we shall please others and not become involved in quarrels or disputes. If we cherish others, we shall be concerned to help rather than to harm them, so we shall naturally avoid negative actions. Instead, we shall practise positive actions, such as love, patience, and generosity, and thus create the cause to gain a precious human life in the future.

If we make cherishing others our main practice, we shall gradually develop very special minds of great compassion and bodhichitta and, as a result, we shall eventually come to enjoy the ultimate happiness of full enlightenment.

MEDITATION

As the preparatory practice, we recite *Prayers for Meditation* while concentrating on the meaning. Then we engage in the following contemplation:

> *The precious mind that cherishes all living beings protects both myself and others from suffering, brings happiness, and fulfils our wishes.*

Having repeatedly contemplated this point, we make the strong determination: "I must always cherish all living beings." This determination is the object of our meditation. We then hold this without forgetting it; our mind should remain on this determination single-pointedly for as long as possible. If we lose the object of our meditation, we renew it by immediately remembering our determination or by repeating the contemplation.

At the end of the meditation session, we dedicate the virtues accumulated from this meditation practice towards our realization of cherishing others and the attainment of enlightenment for the happiness of all living beings.

During the meditation break, we never forget our determination and always put it into practice. We should always keep in mind the great advantages of cherishing others, and continually improve our consideration, respect, and love for them.

13. EXCHANGING SELF WITH OTHERS

The purpose of this meditation is to exchange self with others, which means changing the object of our cherishing so that we give up cherishing ourself and cherish only others.

MEDITATION

As the preparatory practice, we recite *Prayers for Meditation* while concentrating on the meaning. Then we engage in the following contemplation:

> *Since beginningless time, in life after life, I have been a slave to my self-cherishing mind. I have trusted it implicitly and obeyed its every command, believing that the way to solve my problems and find happiness is to put myself before everyone else. I have worked so hard and for so long for my own sake, but what do I have to show for it? Have I solved all my problems and found the lasting happiness I desire?* No. *It is clear that pursuing my own selfish interests has deceived me. After having indulged my self-cherishing for so many lives, now is the time to realize that it simply does not work. Now is the time to switch the object of my cherishing from myself to all living beings.*

Having repeatedly contemplated these points, we make the strong determination: "I must abandon self-cherishing and cherish only others." This determination is the object of our meditation. We then hold this without forgetting it; our mind should remain on this determination single-pointedly for as long as possible. If we lose the object of our meditation, we renew it by immediately remembering our determination or by repeating the contemplation.

At the end of the meditation session, we dedicate the virtues accumulated from this meditation practice towards our realization of exchanging self with others and the attainment of enlightenment for the happiness of all living beings.

During the meditation break, we maintain the determination made in meditation and put it into practice. We should try not to follow our habitual self-cherishing attitude, but instead cherish others sincerely. When we are familiar with exchanging self with others, we shall be able to accept happily any pain or difficulty, such as illness, loss, or criticism, and to offer all our success and good conditions to others.

Victory over the inner

enemy of delusions

14. GREAT COMPASSION

Great compassion is a mind that sincerely wishes to liberate all living beings from suffering. If, on the basis of cherishing all living beings, we contemplate their physical suffering and mental pain, their inability to fulfil their wishes, their lack of freedom, and how, by engaging in negative actions, they sow seeds for future suffering, we shall develop deep compassion for them. We need to empathize with them and feel their pain as keenly as we feel our own.

No one actually wants to suffer, yet living beings create the causes of suffering because they are controlled by their delusions. We should therefore feel equal compassion for all living beings – for those who are creating the causes of suffering, as much as for those who are already suffering the consequences of their unskilful actions. There is not a single living being who is not a suitable object of our compassion.

Living beings suffer because they take samsaric contaminated rebirths. Human beings have no choice but to experience immense human sufferings because they have taken human rebirth, which is contaminated by the inner poison of delusions. Similarly, animals have to experience animal suffering, and hungry spirits and hell beings have to experience all the sufferings of their respective realms. If living beings were to experience all this suffering for just one single life, it would not be so bad, but the cycle of suffering continues life after life, endlessly.

MEDITATION

As the preparatory practice, we recite *Prayers for Meditation* while concentrating on the meaning. We imagine that our parents of this life are beside us, and that they are surrounded by all living beings of the six realms in human aspect. Then, while focusing on all these living beings, we engage in the following contemplation:

> *I cannot bear the suffering of these countless mother beings. Trapped in the prison of samsara, they have to experience again and again, in life after life, endlessly, the immense sufferings of birth, sickness, ageing, and death, having to part with what they like, having to encounter what they do not like, and failing to satisfy their desires.*

Having repeatedly contemplated this point, we generate a strong wish to release all living beings from contaminated rebirth and suffering. This wish is the object of our meditation. We then hold this mind of great, or universal, compassion without forgetting it; our mind should remain on it single-pointedly for as long as possible. If we lose the object of our meditation, we renew it by immediately remembering our wish to release all living beings from suffering or by repeating the contemplation.

At the end of the meditation session, we dedicate the virtues accumulated from this meditation practice towards our realization of great compassion and the attainment of enlightenment for the happiness of all living beings.

During the meditation break, we try to maintain a compassionate heart day and night. Whenever we see or hear of others' suffering, we should try to strengthen our compassion. We must also try to help in practical ways wherever possible. For example, we can rescue animals whose lives are in danger, comfort those who are distressed, or relieve the pain of those who are sick.

15. TAKING

The purpose of this meditation is to purify our mind of self-cherishing and negative actions, to accumulate great merit, and, in particular, to strengthen our compassionate activities. "Taking", in this context, means taking the suffering of others upon ourself – both mentally and physically – motivated by great compassion. During meditation, we mentally take the suffering of others upon ourself, using imagination. Having gained deep experience of this meditation, we shall then be able happily to accept our own suffering in order to release all other living beings from their suffering. In this way, we are physically taking the suffering of others upon ourself.

MEDITATION

As the preparatory practice, we recite *Prayers for Meditation* while concentrating on the meaning. Then we engage in the following practice:

We begin by generating the superior intention: "I myself will liberate all living beings from their suffering." Motivated by this superior intention, we pray: "May all the suffering, fears, and obstacles of every living being ripen upon me, and may they thereby be freed from all problems." We then strongly believe that the suffering, fears, and obstacles of all living beings gather in the aspect of black smoke, which dissolves into our heart, destroying our self-cherishing mind and freeing all living beings from their suffering.

This belief is the object of our meditation. We then hold this without forgetting it; our mind should remain on this belief single-pointedly for as long as possible. If we lose the object of our meditation, we renew it by immediately remembering our belief or by repeating the practice.

At the end of the meditation session, we dedicate the virtues accumulated from this meditation practice towards our realization of taking and the attainment of enlightenment for the happiness of all living beings.

During the meditation break, we put our superior intention – the wish to take the suffering of others upon ourself – into practice. We should alleviate others' suffering whenever we can and happily accept our own suffering as a method to release all other living beings from their suffering. In this way, both our compassion and our merit will increase, our self-cherishing will gradually diminish, and the power of our compassionate activities will strengthen.

16. WISHING LOVE

Having generated affectionate and cherishing love for all living beings, if we now contemplate how living beings lack true happiness we shall naturally develop wishing love – the strong wish that all beings experience pure and everlasting happiness. The main purpose of this meditation is to gain the actual power to bestow pure happiness upon all living beings.

MEDITATION

As the preparatory practice, we recite *Prayers for Meditation* while concentrating on the meaning. Then, focusing on all living beings, we engage in the following contemplation:

> *These living beings wish to be happy all the time, but they do not know how to fulfil this wish. The happiness they experience from worldly enjoyments is not real happiness – it is just changing suffering, a temporary reduction of previous manifest suffering. None of these countless living beings experiences real and everlasting happiness.*

Having repeatedly contemplated this point, we generate the strong wish that all living beings experience real and everlasting happiness. This wish is the object of our meditation. We then hold this without forgetting it; our mind should remain on this wish single-pointedly for as long as possible. If we lose the object of our meditation, we renew it by immediately remembering our wish for all living beings to experience happiness or by repeating the contemplation.

At the end of the meditation session, we dedicate the virtues accumulated from this meditation practice towards our realization of wishing love and the attainment of enlightenment for the happiness of all living beings.

During the meditation break, we always maintain our wishing love and, with this pure intention, make prayers and dedicate our virtues for all living beings to find real and everlasting happiness. We should continually strive to improve our wisdom and compassion so that we can gain the actual power to bestow pure happiness upon all living beings.

17. GIVING

The purpose of this meditation is to learn how to put our wishing love into practice. In this meditation, we give pure happiness to all living beings, using our imagination. By putting this meditation into practice, we shall gain the actual ability to bestow pure and everlasting happiness upon all living beings.

MEDITATION

As the preparatory practice, we recite *Prayers for Meditation* while concentrating on the meaning. Then, focusing on all living beings, we engage in the following practice:

We first think: "All these mother living beings are seeking happiness in life after life. They all want to be happy, but there is no real happiness anywhere in samsara. I will now give them the supreme happiness of permanent inner peace."

We then imagine that through the power of our pure intention of wishing love and great accumulation of merit, our body transforms into the nature of a wishfulfilling jewel, which has the power to fulfil the wishes of each and every living being. Infinite light rays radiate from our body and pervade the entire universe, reaching the bodies and minds of all living beings and bestowing upon them the supreme happiness of permanent inner peace. We strongly believe that all living beings experience this inner peace.

This belief is the object of our meditation. We then hold this without forgetting it; our mind should remain on this belief single-pointedly for as long as possible. If we lose the object of our meditation, we renew it by immediately remembering our belief or by repeating the practice.

At the end of the meditation session, we dedicate the virtues accumulated from this meditation practice towards our realization of the practice of giving and the attainment of enlightenment for the happiness of all living beings.

During the meditation break, we try to practise giving love, giving Dharma, giving fearlessness, and giving material things. Whenever we can, we try to be of service to others. We should also make prayers and dedicate our merit so that all living beings obtain pure happiness. In this way, our wishing love, as well as our merit, will quickly increase.

18. BODHICHITTA

"Bodhichitta" literally means "mind of enlightenment" – "bodhi" is the Sanskrit word for "enlightenment" and "chitta" the word for "mind". Bodhichitta is defined as a mind, motivated by compassion for all living beings, that spontaneously seeks enlightenment. It is born from great compassion, which itself depends upon cherishing love. Cherishing love can be likened to a field, compassion to the seeds, taking and giving to perfect conditions for enabling the seeds to grow, and bodhichitta to the harvest.

Bodhichitta is the supreme good heart. This profoundly compassionate mind is the very essence of spiritual training. Developing the good heart of bodhichitta enables us to perfect all our virtues, solve all our problems, fulfil all our wishes, and develop the power to help others in the most appropriate and beneficial ways. Bodhichitta is the best friend we can have and the greatest quality we can develop.

MEDITATION

As the preparatory practice, we recite *Prayers for Meditation* while concentrating on the meaning. Then we recall the superior intention generated in the meditations on taking and giving and engage in the following contemplation:

I have assumed responsibility for liberating all living beings from suffering, but how can I do this without first attaining enlightenment myself? Only enlightened beings have the power to protect all living beings and to bestow upon them pure and everlasting happiness. Therefore, to fulfil my wish to liberate all living beings from their suffering, I must become a Buddha, a fully enlightened being.

Having repeatedly contemplated these points, we generate the strong wish to attain enlightenment to free all living beings from their suffering. This wish is the object of our meditation. We then hold this without forgetting it; our mind should remain on this wish single-pointedly for as long as possible. If we lose the object of our meditation, we renew it by immediately remembering our wish or by repeating the contemplation.

At the end of the meditation session, we dedicate the virtues accumulated from this meditation practice towards our realization of bodhichitta and the attainment of enlightenment for the happiness of all living beings.

During the meditation break, we try to maintain the precious mind of bodhichitta day and night. In particular, we should try to ensure that whatever actions we undertake are motivated by bodhichitta. In this way, all our actions become powerful causes of Buddhahood.

Having gained some experience of bodhichitta, we should bring it to completion by practising the three higher trainings of the Mahayana: training in the perfection of moral discipline by keeping the Bodhisattva vows purely; training in the perfection of mental stabilization by striving to attain tranquil abiding; and training in the perfection of wisdom by developing superior seeing. A detailed explanation of the Bodhisattva vows can be found in the book *The Bodhisattva Vow*.

Strive to become a pure being

19. TRANQUIL ABIDING

Bodhichitta and the wisdom directly realizing emptiness are like the two wings of a bird that can carry us to our destination, the ground of enlightenment. To realize emptiness directly, we need to attain tranquil abiding. Without tranquil abiding, our mind is unstable, like a candle flame exposed to the wind, and so we are not able to realize clearly and directly subtle objects such as emptiness. It is not just the direct realization of emptiness that depends upon tranquil abiding; we also need tranquil abiding to attain spontaneous realizations of renunciation and bodhichitta, and pure clairvoyance and miracle powers.

In general, whenever we experience pure concentration on any of the objects of the twenty-one meditations, our mind abides in a tranquil state, free from distractions. This is the function of pure concentration. However, actual tranquil abiding is a special concentration that is attained by completing the training in the nine levels of concentration known as the "nine mental abidings", and that is conjoined with a special bliss of mental and physical suppleness. To train in tranquil abiding, we first need to choose an object of meditation. We can use any one of the objects of the twenty-one meditations. If we choose an object such as equanimity, love, compassion, or bodhichitta, we first transform our mind into that particular state of mind by using the appropriate contemplations, and then hold that state of mind with single-pointed concentration. If we choose an object such as emptiness, impermanence, or the preciousness of this human life, we first attain a clear mental image of the object by relying upon the appropriate contemplations, and then concentrate single-pointedly on that image.

The instructions that follow explain how to begin to train in tranquil abiding using great compassion as the object. If we choose a different object, we can modify the instructions accordingly.

MEDITATION

As the preparatory practice, we recite *Prayers for Meditation* while concentrating on the meaning. Then we engage in the following practice:

> *Remembering our affectionate and cherishing love for all living beings, we think: "I cannot bear that these countless mother beings, trapped in the prison of samsara, have to experience again and again, in life after life, endlessly, the immense sufferings of birth, sickness, ageing, and death, having to part with what they like, having to encounter what they do not like, and failing to satisfy their desires."*

When as a result of this contemplation a strong feeling of compassion for all living beings arises in our mind, we have found the object of our tranquil abiding meditation. Having transformed our mind into compassion, we then stop contemplating and, with strong concentration, hold this mind of compassion for all living beings.

This concentration is the first of the nine mental abidings. When the object fades, or our mind wanders to another object, we return to the contemplation to bring the object back to mind. Then once again we discontinue our contemplation and hold the object with single-pointed concentration. We continue in this way, alternating between contemplation and meditation, for the rest of the session.

We continue to improve our concentration in this way until we are able to remain concentrated on our object for five minutes. At this point, we shall have advanced to the second mental abiding. By continually improving our concentration, we shall attain tranquil abiding.

At the end of the meditation session, we dedicate the virtues accumulated from this meditation practice towards our realization of tranquil abiding and the attainment of enlightenment for the happiness of all living beings.

During the meditation break, our principal practice is to observe pure moral discipline carefully by relying upon mindfulness and conscientiousness. In this way, we avoid distracting thoughts that obstruct our training in tranquil abiding. Again and again we should think about the benefits of attaining tranquil abiding to increase our enthusiasm for the practice, and to improve our understanding we should read authentic instructions on tranquil abiding such as those found in *Joyful Path of Good Fortune* and *Meaningful to Behold*.

Once we have attained the fourth mental abiding, we are ready to do a strict retreat on tranquil abiding. In some cases, at this stage it is possible to attain actual tranquil abiding within six months. For our retreat on tranquil abiding to be successful, we need to find a suitable place that is very quiet and has all the necessary conditions. We must have few desires and be able to remain content all the time.

During the retreat, we should refrain from worldly activities and keep moral discipline purely, thereby reducing distracting conceptions. In brief, we must free ourself from all obstacles to developing concentration, and obtain all conducive internal and external conditions.

20. SUPERIOR SEEING

In this context, "superior seeing" refers to a profound wisdom that sees the way things really are and which is attained through tranquil abiding. With this wisdom, we are able to abandon our self-grasping ignorance – the root of all our suffering – and all our mistaken appearances, so that we can enjoy the supreme inner peace of enlightenment. The object of this wisdom is emptiness. Therefore, in this session we emphasize meditation on emptiness.

Emptiness is not nothingness but is the real nature of phenomena; it is the way things really are. Emptiness is the way things exist as opposed to the way they appear. We naturally believe that the things we see around us, such as tables, chairs, and houses, are truly existent, because we believe that they exist in exactly the way that they appear. However, the way things appear to our senses is deceptive and completely contradictory to the way in which they actually exist. Things appear to exist from their own side, without depending upon our mind. We feel that this book that appears to our mind, for example, can exist without our mind; we do not feel that our mind is in any way involved in bringing the book into existence. This way of existing independent of our mind is variously called "true existence", "inherent existence", and "existence from its own side".

Although things appear directly to our senses to be truly, or inherently, existent, in reality all phenomena lack true, or inherent, existence. This book, our body, we ourself, and the entire universe are in reality just appearances to mind, like things seen in a dream. If we dream of an elephant, the elephant appears vividly in all its detail – we can see it, hear it, smell it, and touch it – but when we wake up we realize that it was just an appearance to mind. We do not wonder, "Where is the elephant now?", because we understand that it was simply a projection of our mind and had no existence outside our mind. When the dream awareness that apprehended the elephant ceased, the elephant did not go anywhere – it simply disappeared, for it was just an appearance to the mind and did not exist separately from the mind. Buddha said that the same is true for all phenomena; they are mere appearances to mind, totally dependent upon the minds that perceive them.

The world we experience when we are awake and the world we experience when we are dreaming are very similar, for both are mere appearances to mind that arise from our karma. If we want to say that the dream world is false, we also have to say that the waking world is false; and if we want to say that the waking world is true, we also have to say that the dream world is true. The only difference between them is that the dream world is an appearance to our subtle dreaming mind whereas the waking world is an appearance to our gross waking mind. The dream world exists only for as long as the dream awareness to which it appears exists, and the waking world exists only for as long as the waking awareness to which it appears exists. When we die, our gross waking minds dissolve into our very subtle mind and the world we experienced when we were alive simply disappears. The world as others perceive it will continue, but our personal world will disappear as completely and irrevocably as the world of last night's dream.

Buddha said that all phenomena are like illusions. There are many different types of illusion, such as mirages, rainbows, or drug-induced hallucinations. In ancient times, there used to be magicians who would cast a spell over their audience, causing them to see objects, such as a piece of wood, as something else, such as a tiger. Those deceived by the spell would see what appeared to be a real tiger and develop fear, but those who arrived after the spell had been cast would simply see a piece of wood. What all illusions have in common is that the way they appear does not coincide with the way they exist. Buddha likened all phenomena to illusions because, through the force of the imprints of self-grasping ignorance accumulated since beginningless time, whatever appears to our mind naturally appears to be truly existent and we instinctively assent to this appearance, but in reality everything is totally empty of true existence. Like a mirage that appears to be water but is not in fact water, things appear in a deceptive way. Not understanding their real nature, we are fooled by appearances, and grasp at books and tables, bodies and worlds as truly existent. This grasping mind is self-grasping. The result of grasping at phenomena in this way is that we develop self-cherishing, attachment, hatred, jealousy, and other delusions, our mind becomes agitated and unbalanced, and our inner peace is destroyed. We are like travellers in a desert who exhaust themselves running after mirages, or like someone walking down a road at night mistaking the shadows of the trees for criminals or wild animals waiting to attack.

To understand how all phenomena are empty of true, or inherent, existence, we should consider our own body. Once we have understood how our body lacks true existence, we can easily apply the same reasoning to other objects.

On one level we know our body very well – we know whether it is healthy or unhealthy, tall or short, and so forth. However, we never examine it more deeply, asking ourself: "What precisely is my body? Where is my body? What is its real nature?" If we did examine our body in this way, we would not be able to find it – instead of finding our body, the result of this examination would be that our body disappears. This clearly shows that our body is empty of true or inherent existence, and this is also true of our I, our world, and all other phenomena.

MEDITATION

As the preparatory practice, we recite *Prayers for Meditation* while concentrating on the meaning. Then we recall the meaning of the above explanation and think:

> *My body is empty of true, or inherent, existence because, when I search for it, it disappears like a mirage.*

Having repeatedly contemplated this point, when we see clearly that our body is empty of true existence we have found the object of our meditation, the emptiness of our body. We then hold this emptiness without forgetting it; our mind should remain on the emptiness of a truly existent body single-pointedly for as long as possible. If we lose the object of our meditation, we renew it by immediately remembering the emptiness of our body or by repeating the contemplation.

At the end of the meditation session, we dedicate the virtues accumulated from this meditation practice towards our realization of superior seeing and the attainment of enlightenment for the happiness of all living beings.

Having gained some experience of the meditation of the emptiness of our body, we can then apply the above contemplation and meditation to our I, our world, and all other phenomena. In this way, we meditate on the emptiness of all phenomena, and we shall develop a special feeling that all our ordinary daily appearances are dissolving into an ocean of emptiness. Through this, our self-grasping and other delusions will gradually diminish and our inner peace will continually increase.

During the meditation break, we try to recognize that whatever appears to our mind lacks true or inherent existence. In a dream, things appear vividly to the dreamer, but, when the dreamer wakes, he or she immediately realizes that the objects that appeared in the dream were just mental appearances that did not exist from their own side. We should view all phenomena in a similar way. Though they appear vividly to our mind, they lack inherent existence.

A detailed explanation of emptiness can be found in *Transform Your Life*, and a traditional explanation of how to contemplate and meditate on the emptiness of the I and the body is given in Appendix VI.

Complete the Bodhisattva's path

21. RELYING UPON A SPIRITUAL GUIDE

The purpose of this meditation is to enable us to receive the powerful blessings of all enlightened beings through our Spiritual Guide so that our meditation practice will be successful. Sick people rely upon doctors who temporarily liberate them from particular illnesses, so there is no doubt that we need to rely upon a qualified Spiritual Guide who will lead us to permanent liberation from the sufferings of both inner and outer sickness.

By relying upon a qualified Spiritual Guide with strong faith, we can remove all our confusion about Dharma, increase our Dharma wisdom, and receive the powerful blessings of all enlightened beings. Buddha said that relying upon a qualified Spiritual Guide is the root of the spiritual path, and that by relying upon our Spiritual Guide we shall receive the following benefits:

1 He or she will lead us along the spiritual path, which is the only way to solve all our problems and make our life meaningful.
2 His or her blessings will gradually draw us closer to the attainment of full enlightenment.
3 All the Buddhas will be delighted with us.
4 We shall be protected from harm caused by humans or non-humans.
5 We shall find it easy to abandon our delusions and non-virtuous actions.
6 Our practical experience of the spiritual path will increase.

7 We shall never be born in lower realms.
8 In all our future lives, we shall meet qualified Spiritual Guides.
9 All our virtuous wishes for beneficial conditions within samsara, as well as for liberation and enlightenment, will be fulfilled.

MEDITATION

As the preparatory practice, we recite *Prayers for Meditation* while concentrating on the meaning. Then we engage in the actual meditation:

> *Having repeatedly contemplated all the benefits of relying upon a Spiritual Guide mentioned above, we make the strong determination: "I must sincerely rely upon a Spiritual Guide."*

This determination is the object of our meditation. We then hold this without forgetting it; our mind should remain on this determination single-pointedly for as long as possible. If we lose the object of our meditation, we renew it by immediately remembering our determination or by repeating the contemplation.

At the end of the meditation session, we dedicate the virtues accumulated from this meditation practice towards our realization of relying upon a Spiritual Guide and the attainment of enlightenment for the happiness of all living beings.

During the meditation break, we put our determination into practice. A detailed explanation of the qualifications of a Spiritual Guide and how to become a qualified student can be found in *Joyful Path of Good Fortune* and *Great Treasury of Merit*.

This meditation can be either the first or the last of the twenty-one meditations. In this book, I have chosen to put it last.

The ultimate goal is enlightenment

Conclusion

Having developed the supreme good heart of bodhichitta, we should engage in the practices of giving, moral discipline, patience, effort, concentration, and wisdom. When motivated by bodhichitta, these practices are called the "six perfections". By training in the six perfections, and especially in the perfections of concentration and wisdom, we shall fulfil our bodhichitta wishes.

Appendix I

Prayers for Meditation

BRIEF PREPARATORY PRAYERS FOR MEDITATION

Prayers for Meditation

Going for refuge

I and all sentient beings, until we achieve enlightenment,
Go for refuge to Buddha, Dharma, and Sangha.
(3x, 7x, 100x, or more)

Generating bodhichitta

Through the virtues I collect by giving and other perfections,
May I become a Buddha for the benefit of all. (3x)

Generating the four immeasurables

May everyone be happy,
May everyone be free from misery,
May no one ever be separated from their happiness,
May everyone have equanimity, free from hatred and attachment.

Visualizing the Field for Accumulating Merit

In the space before me is the living Buddha Shakyamuni surrounded by all the Buddhas and Bodhisattvas, like the full moon surrounded by stars.

Prayer of seven limbs

With my body, speech, and mind, humbly I prostrate,
And make offerings both set out and imagined.
I confess my wrong deeds from all time,
And rejoice in the virtues of all.
Please stay until samsara ceases,
And turn the Wheel of Dharma for us.
I dedicate all virtues to great enlightenment.

Offering the mandala

The ground sprinkled with perfume and spread with flowers,
The Great Mountain, four lands, sun and moon,
Seen as a Buddha Land and offered thus,
May all beings enjoy such Pure Lands.

I offer without any sense of loss
The objects that give rise to my attachment, hatred, and confusion,
My friends, enemies, and strangers, our bodies and enjoyments;
Please accept these and bless me to be released directly from the three poisons.

IDAM GURU RATNA MANDALAKAM NIRYATAYAMI

Prayer of the Stages of the Path

The path begins with strong reliance
On my kind Teacher, source of all good;
O Bless me with this understanding
To follow him with great devotion.

This human life with all its freedoms,
Extremely rare, with so much meaning;
O Bless me with this understanding
All day and night to seize its essence.

My body, like a water bubble,
Decays and dies so very quickly;
After death come results of karma,
Just like the shadow of a body.

With this firm knowledge and remembrance
Bless me to be extremely cautious,
Always avoiding harmful actions
And gathering abundant virtue.

Samsara's pleasures are deceptive,
Give no contentment, only torment;
So please bless me to strive sincerely
To gain the bliss of perfect freedom.

O Bless me so that from this pure thought
Come mindfulness and greatest caution,
To keep as my essential practice
The doctrine's root, the Pratimoksha.

Just like myself all my kind mothers
Are drowning in samsara's ocean;
O So that I may soon release them,
Bless me to train in bodhichitta.

But I cannot become a Buddha
By this alone without three ethics;
So bless me with the strength to practise
The Bodhisattva's ordination.

By pacifying my distractions
And analyzing perfect meanings,
Bless me to quickly gain the union
Of special insight and quiescence.

When I become a pure container
Through common paths, bless me to enter
The essence practice of good fortune,
The supreme vehicle, Vajrayana.

The two attainments both depend on
My sacred vows and my commitments;
Bless me to understand this clearly
And keep them at the cost of my life.

By constant practice in four sessions,
The way explained by holy Teachers,
O Bless me to gain both the stages,
Which are the essence of the Tantras.

May those who guide me on the good path,
And my companions all have long lives;
Bless me to pacify completely
All obstacles, outer and inner.

May I always find perfect Teachers,
And take delight in holy Dharma,
Accomplish all grounds and paths swiftly,
And gain the state of Vajradhara.

Receiving blessings and purifying

From the hearts of all the holy beings, streams of light and nectar flow down, granting blessings and purifying.

At this point we begin the actual contemplation and meditation. After the meditation we dedicate our merit while reciting the following prayers:

Dedication prayers

Through the virtues I have collected
By practising the stages of the path,
May all living beings find the opportunity
To practise in the same way.

May everyone experience
The happiness of humans and gods,
And quickly attain enlightenment,
So that samsara is finally extinguished.

Colophon: These prayers were compiled from traditional sources by Geshe Kelsang Gyatso Rinpoche.

Appendix II

A Commentary to the Preparatory Practices

A Commentary to the Preparatory Practices

PREPARING FOR MEDITATION

We all have the potential to gain realizations of each of the twenty-one meditation practices in this book. These potentials are like seeds in the field of our mind, and our meditation practice is like cultivating these seeds. However, our meditation practice will be successful only if we make good preparations beforehand.

If we want to cultivate external crops, we begin by making careful preparations. First, we remove from the soil anything that might obstruct their growth, such as stones and weeds. Second, we enrich the soil with compost or fertilizer to give it the strength to sustain growth. Third, we provide warm, moist conditions to enable the seeds to germinate and the plants to grow. In the same way, to cultivate our inner crops of Dharma realizations we must also begin by making careful preparations. First, we must purify our mind to eliminate the negative karma we have accumulated in the past, because, if we do not purify this karma, it will obstruct the growth of Dharma realizations. Second, we need to give our mind the strength to support the growth of Dharma realizations by accumulating merit. Third, we need to activate and sustain the growth of Dharma realizations by receiving the blessings of the holy beings.

It is very important to receive blessings. For example, if we are growing outer crops, even if we remove the weeds and fertilize the soil, we shall not be able to grow anything if we do not provide warmth and moisture. These germinate the seeds, sustain the growth of the plants, and finally ripen the crop. In the same way, even if we purify our mind and accumulate merit, we shall find it difficult to meet with success in our meditations if we do not receive the blessings of the holy beings. Receiving blessings transforms our mind by activating our virtuous potentials, sustaining the growth of our Dharma realizations, and bringing our Dharma practice to completion.

From this, we can see that there are three essential preparations for successful meditation: purifying negativities, accumulating merit, and receiving blessings. The brief preparatory practices that now follow contain the essence of these three preparations.

Cleaning the environment

Before we sit down to meditate, it is helpful to make sure that the place where we meditate is clean. A clean environment makes the mind clear and fresh. Moreover, during the preparatory practices we invite the Buddhas, Bodhisattvas, and other holy beings to come to our room as a Field for Accumulating Merit, and, as a sign of respect, we ensure that our room is clean and tidy beforehand.

Setting up a shrine

If possible, we should set up a shrine with representations of Buddha's body, speech, and mind. To represent Buddha's body, we place a statue or picture of Buddha in the centre of the shrine. To its right we place a Dharma text, representing Buddha's speech, and to its left we place a stupa, or a picture of a stupa, representing Buddha's mind. Remembering that Buddha's omniscient mind actually enters into these objects, we should feel that we are actually in the presence of the living Buddha and make prostrations and offerings accordingly.

If we like, we can set out actual offerings in front of the shrine, such as rows of seven water bowls, or anything clean and beautiful, such as flowers, incense, candles, honey, cakes, chocolate, or fruit. More information on setting up a shrine and making offerings can be found in *Joyful Path of Good Fortune*.

The meditation posture

When these preparations are completed, we can sit down to meditate. If possible, we should sit in the vajra posture, but, if we are unfamiliar with this, we can sit in any posture that is comfortable. If we cannot sit cross-legged, we can sit on a chair. The most important thing is to have a straight back so that the subtle energy winds in our body can flow freely and keep our mind alert. Our hands should rest just below the navel, with the palms open and facing upwards, the right hand above the left, and the two thumbs gently touching.

Calming the mind

Before beginning the actual preparatory prayers, we should calm our mind by doing breathing meditation. Breathing naturally, we try to concentrate on our breath without being distracted by conceptual thoughts. As we breathe out, we imagine that we exhale all our negativities, obstacles, and distracting thoughts in the form of black smoke. As we breathe in, we imagine that we inhale the blessings of all the holy beings in the form of pure, white light. We continue with this meditation for a few minutes, or until our mind is calm and peaceful. If we like, we can use the special breathing meditation explained in Appendix III.

The remaining preparatory practices are done in conjunction with *Prayers for Meditation*. The purpose of reciting these prayers is to direct our mind to the particular practices. These will now be briefly explained.

Going for refuge We generate fear of the sufferings of samsara in general, and of rebirth in the lower realms in particular; and then, with strong faith that the Three Jewels have the power to protect us from these sufferings, we go for refuge to Buddha, Dharma, and Sangha while reciting the refuge prayer. The actual practice of going for refuge is explained in Meditation 4.

Generating bodhichitta There are two important things to emphasize when we meditate: our motivation at the beginning and our dedication at the end. We should begin by generating the motivation of bodhichitta, the wish to attain Buddhahood to help all living beings. With this motivation, we recite the bodhichitta prayer. Our familiarity with both refuge and bodhichitta will naturally increase as we practise the cycle of twenty-one meditations.

Generating the four immeasurables These are four special states of mind that strengthen our bodhichitta. They are immeasurable love, the wish for all beings to be happy; immeasurable compassion, the wish for all beings to be free from suffering; immeasurable joy, the wish for all beings to attain the everlasting joy of liberation; and immeasurable equanimity, the wish for all beings to be free from unbalanced attitudes such as attachment and anger. They are called "immeasurables" because we generate these minds while thinking of all living beings, who are immeasurable in number.

Visualizing the Field for Accumulating Merit The Field for Accumulating Merit is the assembly of Buddhas, Bodhisattvas, and other holy beings in whom we take refuge and to whom we make prostrations, offerings, confession, and so forth. We imagine that they are all in the space before us, with Buddha Shakyamuni, our main object of visualization, in the centre and all the other holy beings around him, like the full moon surrounded by stars. They are called a "Field for Accumulating Merit" because, by offering the prayer of seven limbs and the mandala to them, we accumulate merit in our minds. At the beginning, we should not expect to be able to visualize the whole assembly; it is sufficient simply to believe that they are all present before us.

Prayer of seven limbs The seven limbs are methods for purifying negativity and accumulating merit. They are: prostrating, making offerings, confessing non-virtue, rejoicing in virtue, beseeching the holy beings to remain, requesting Dharma teachings, and dedicating merit. They are called "limbs" because they support our meditation, which is the main body of our practice. Prostrating, making offerings, rejoicing in virtue, beseeching the holy beings to remain, and requesting Dharma teachings all accumulate merit; confessing non-virtue purifies negativity; and dedicating our merit prevents our virtue from being destroyed.

To prostrate is to show respect. We can show respect with our body by making physical prostrations or simply by placing our hands together at our heart; we can show respect with our speech by reciting verses of praise; and we can show respect with our mind by generating faith towards the holy beings. If possible, we should make all three types of prostration together. This practice also serves to reduce our pride and other strong delusions.

As already mentioned, we can make actual offerings by placing seven or more water bowls in front of our shrine, or by offering anything clean and beautiful, such as flowers, incense, or fruit. If we use our imagination, we can offer jewelled palaces, gardens, scented bathing pools, even entire universes – all completely pure. The Buddhas and Bodhisattvas have no need for our offerings, but making extensive offerings has a very beneficial effect on our mind, creating a vast amount of merit, or good fortune, and counteracting miserliness.

Confession enables us to purify negative actions committed in the past. If we sincerely contemplate and meditate on karma, we shall realize that we have already committed countless heavy negative actions. Fearing the consequences of these actions, we develop a strong wish to purify them. To purify negative actions, we must recognize the faults of these actions and feel regret for having committed them. Regret is not the same as guilt. It is simply a strong wish to purify our mind of the negative energy created by non-virtuous actions. Feeling regret for all the non-virtuous actions we have committed, we confess them to the holy beings. In this way, we receive the purifying blessings of all the Buddhas and Bodhisattvas. With these attitudes of regret and faith, any virtuous actions we engage in serve as purification. If we begin every meditation session with sincere confession, the whole session serves to purify our accumulated negativity. To purify completely a non-virtuous action, we must make a promise not to repeat it. There is little point in confessing our negative actions if we have no intention to refrain from committing them again in the future.

Rejoicing is to appreciate and rejoice in the virtues of ourself and others. Rejoicing in virtue increases our virtuous tendencies and overcomes jealousy and competitiveness. It is one of the easiest ways to create a vast amount of merit. Even lying in bed and rejoicing in the virtuous actions of others is a powerful spiritual practice.

Beseeching our Spiritual Guide and all the other holy beings to remain with us – to guide us and inspire us – helps us to keep a strong connection with our Spiritual Guide in this and future lives.

Requesting the holy beings to turn the Wheel of Dharma, that is, to give Dharma teachings, creates the cause for Dharma to remain in this world and ensures that we shall meet with Dharma in our future lives.

As mentioned before, dedication is very important because it directs the merit we accumulate through our meditation practice towards the attainment of full enlightenment, and prevents it from being destroyed by anger or other non-virtuous minds such as wrong views. We dedicate by generating a strong mental intention that our merit will become a cause of our enlightenment for the benefit of all living beings.

For those who are interested in practising the seven limbs more elaborately, a detailed commentary can be found in *Joyful Path of Good Fortune* and in the second and third chapters of *Meaningful to Behold*.

Offering the mandala The mandala offering is a way to offer the entire universe in visualized form. We imagine that the whole universe transforms into a Buddha's Pure Land, which we offer to the Field of Merit with the prayer that all living beings may soon come to live in such a Pure Land. To make the mandala offering, we visualize that we hold in our hands a vast and circular golden base. In the centre stands Mount Meru, around this are four island continents, and in the space above are the sun and the moon. Everything pure and beautiful is included in the mandala. When we recite the second verse of the mandala offering, we offer everything that stimulates our delusions. We imagine that the people and things to which we are attached, as well as those that cause us to develop hatred and confusion, all transform into pure beings and enjoyments, and we offer them to the Three Jewels. By transforming and offering the objects of the three poisons – attachment, hatred, and confusion – we remove the basis upon which these delusions develop. More detail on offering the mandala can be found in *Joyful Path of Good Fortune, Great Treasury of Merit*, and *Guide to Dakini Land.*

Prayer of the Stages of the Path After purifying negativity and accumulating merit by reciting the prayer of seven limbs and offering the mandala, we now request the holy beings to grant their blessings so that we may receive all the realizations of the stages of the path. We make this request by reciting the *Prayer of the Stages of the Path* while concentrating single-pointedly on its meaning.

Receiving blessings and purifying After making requests by reciting the *Prayer of the Stages of the Path,* we imagine that Buddha Shakyamuni and all the other Buddhas and Bodhisattvas are delighted. Smiling with the love of a father for his dearest child, Buddha radiates rays of light and nectar from his heart, which enter the crown of our head and fill our whole body. This purifies all our hindrances to attaining deep experience of the topic on which we are about to meditate, and makes our mind very clear, positive, and powerful. We should firmly believe that this happens.

Contemplation and meditation Now that we have purified our mind, accumulated merit, and received blessings, we are ready to begin our contemplation and meditation by following the specific instructions given for each meditation.

If, during the course of our meditation, our mind becomes dull or heavy, or if we meet with other difficulties, we should pause from our meditation and make prayers to the holy beings in front of us. We imagine that they answer our prayers with powerful lights and nectars, which flow into our body and immediately dispel our obstacles. We then resume our meditation.

These preparations are extremely important for successful meditation. If we wish to spend longer on them, we can recite a slightly more extensive preparatory prayer called *Essence of Good Fortune,* which can be found in *Joyful Path of Good Fortune.* If we wish, we can emphasize going for refuge by reciting the refuge prayer hundreds of times, or we can accumulate merit by making many mandala offerings, or we can emphasize purification by making prostrations to the Thirty-five Confession Buddhas, as explained in the book *The Bodhisattva Vow*. Sometimes, if we wish, we can devote the entire session to the preparatory practices.

Dedication At the end of our session, we imagine that all the holy beings melt into light and dissolve through the crown of our head. We feel as if our body, speech, and mind have become one with Buddha's body, speech, and mind. Then, while reciting the dedication prayers, we dedicate the merit we have accumulated from practising the preparations, contemplating, and meditating to the happiness of all living beings.

It is not enough for the preparatory practices to be mere verbal recitation or something we engage in only during our meditation session. Instead, the practices of making prostrations, making offerings – especially the mandala offering – confessing non-virtue, rejoicing in virtue, beseeching the holy beings to remain, requesting Dharma teachings, and dedicating merit should be integrated practically into every moment of our daily life. In this way, our good fortune will continually grow, our mind will become pure and clear, and our spiritual activities will be powerful and effective.

Appendix III

A Special Breathing Meditation

OM

Symbol of the body of all Buddhas

A Special Breathing Meditation

Generally, the purpose of breathing meditation is to calm the mind and reduce distractions before engaging in a practical meditation, such as any of the twenty-one meditations described in this book. A simple breathing meditation such as the one explained on pages 11–3 will help us to do this, but the meditation explained here also performs many other functions. It helps us to improve our motivation, to develop a good heart and a controlled mind, and to increase our energy for practising Dharma. It is also a special method for ripening our Buddha seeds and for preparing us for Highest Yoga Tantra meditation.

In this meditation, we combine our breathing with the recitation of the mantra OM AH HUM, which is called the "mantra of all Buddhas". There are many different mantras, but they are all contained within these three letters. All Buddhas are contained within three groups: vajra body, vajra speech, and vajra mind. The mantra of vajra body is OM, the mantra of vajra speech is AH, and the mantra of

AH

Symbol of the speech of

all Buddhas

vajra mind is HUM. Therefore, if we recite these three letters with faith, we shall receive the blessings of the body, speech, and mind of all Buddhas.

A Buddha is someone who is completely free from all faults and limitations and who has developed all good qualities to perfection. Therefore, a Buddha possesses special qualities of body, speech, and mind that are not possessed by ordinary beings. When we recite this mantra, we should have deep faith in these qualities and generate a strong wish to develop them ourself.

Even the most exalted ordinary beings, such as kings and queens, possess only one body, but a Buddha possesses many bodies. A Buddha's actual body is his or her omniscient mind. This is called the "Truth Body". Because only other enlightened beings can see this body, the Truth Body manifests a subtle Form Body called the "Enjoyment Body". This body, however, is very subtle, and can be seen only by Superior Bodhisattvas, those who have a direct realization of emptiness. To be able to communicate directly with ordinary beings, the Enjoyment Body emanates countless gross Form Bodies called "Emanation Bodies". There are two types of Emanation Body: Supreme Emanation Bodies and Emanation Bodies appearing as ordinary beings. The former can be seen only by those with pure minds and pure karma, but the latter can be seen by anyone. According to Mahayana Buddhism, Buddha's Emanation Bodies pervade the whole world, although they are not usually recognized by ordinary beings. Ordinary beings have ordinary minds and so they see everything, even an emanation of Buddha, as ordinary.

HUM

Symbol of the mind of

all Buddhas

A Buddha's speech also possesses many good qualities. Unlike the speech of ordinary beings, which does not have much power, the speech of a Buddha has the power to help all living beings. Everyone wishes to be free from suffering and to experience pure happiness, and Buddha's speech explains how to fulfil this wish. Even though we are constantly seeking happiness, we never find it. Buddha explains that this is because we are trapped in samsara. True happiness can be found only outside samsara. If we want to experience this happiness, we must escape from samsara by relying upon the spiritual paths taught by Buddha. Then we shall experience a permanent cessation of suffering, and uninterrupted peace and happiness. Buddha's speech, therefore, is the key that releases us from the prison of samsara and fulfils our wish for happiness.

Buddhas also possess many unique qualities of mind. A Buddha's mind is completely free from ignorance and its imprints, like a sky free from clouds. Because their minds are utterly unobstructed, Buddhas know directly and simultaneously all phenomena of the past, present, and future. The mind of a Buddha is the highest level of mental development.

We all have the seeds of a Buddha's body, speech, and mind, and, if we practise pure spiritual paths, we can cause these seeds to ripen and accomplish these special qualities. If we continue to improve our present minds of love, compassion, and bodhichitta, we shall become a Bodhisattva. If we then continue to train in pure spiritual paths, eventually we shall become a Buddha. In Mahayana Buddhism, our way of relying upon Buddha is not simply asking Buddha to help us, but striving ourself to become a Buddha to be able to help others. Therefore, we should try gradually to reduce our faults of body, speech, and mind and to develop all good qualities instead. As our faults diminish and our good qualities increase, we shall come closer and closer to Buddhahood. Eventually, we shall become a fully enlightened being. Many thousands of Mahayana practitioners in the past have attained enlightenment in this way.

Contemplating these points, we should think:

> *How wonderful it would be if I became a Buddha and attained the good qualities of a Buddha's body, speech, and mind! At the moment I have no power to help others but, if I become a Buddha, I shall be able to help all living beings without exception. Therefore, I must become a Buddha.*

This motivation is bodhichitta. With this motivation, we should engage in the recitation of the mantra OM AH HUM, while remembering its meaning. Until we become used to the mantra, we should recite it verbally. Then we can combine it with breathing meditation.

To do this, we breathe gently and naturally through both nostrils. As we inhale, we mentally recite OM. We then hold the breath briefly at our heart and mentally recite AH. Then, as we gently exhale, we mentally recite HUM. We repeat this cycle as many times as we wish, all the time remembering the meaning of the mantra with a mind of faith. The "heart" that is referred to here is the spiritual heart, not the physical heart. It is located in the centre of the chest. To begin with, we shall be able to hold our breath only for a short time, but, with familiarity, we shall be able to hold it for longer and longer without discomfort.

This meditation produces many good results. It calms our mind and causes our distracting conceptions to subside. It strengthens the life-supporting wind at our heart, thereby increasing our lifespan and protecting us from premature death. Because we do this meditation with the motivation to attain the good qualities of a Buddha's body, speech, and mind, we are also training in bodhichitta, accumulating merit, and receiving Buddha's blessings. It causes our Buddha seeds to ripen, and it prepares us for Highest Yoga Tantra meditation, making it easy to attain completion stage realizations in the future. Therefore, it is far more powerful than ordinary breathing meditation.

The effects of this practice remain even when we rise from meditation. If we do this meditation regularly, we shall find that our mind gradually becomes more positive and more controlled. It will become like a well-trained horse that does whatever the rider wishes. If we wish to meditate, our mind will remain on the object without distraction. If we wish to do prostrations, it will engage happily, without procrastination or laziness. As our mind becomes more controlled, we shall find it easier to refrain from negative actions of body, speech, and mind, and to practise virtue. We shall experience peace and happiness day and night, in life after life; and be able to share the benefits of this experience with others. This is the real meaning of the Buddhist way of life.

Understanding the many benefits of this special breathing meditation, we should try to do it whenever we can.

Appendix IV

A Suggested Retreat Schedule

A Suggested Retreat Schedule

When we do retreat on the twenty-one meditations, it is best if our retreat is at least one week long. If possible, we should do four sessions each day. The first session should be early in the morning, the second before lunch, the third in the late afternoon, and the fourth in the evening. We can make the sessions as long as we wish, from half an hour up to two hours each. We should begin each session with the preparatory practices and then engage in the contemplations and meditations according to the sequence suggested below. At the end of each session, we should dedicate our merit for the welfare of all living beings, and in between sessions we should try to engage in the subsequent practices with strong mindfulness. If the retreat is longer than one week, we can repeat the cycle each week. In this way, each week we shall cover all twenty-one meditations, from our precious human life to relying upon a Spiritual Guide.

DAY ONE

Session 1	Meditation 1 – Our precious human life
Session 2	Meditation 2 – Death and impermanence
Session 3	Meditation 3 & 4 – The danger of lower rebirth and refuge practice
Session 4	Meditations 5 – Actions and their effects

DAY TWO

Session 1	Meditation 6 – Developing renunciation, using the first four contemplations: birth, sickness, ageing, and death
Session 2	Meditation 6 – Developing renunciation, using the remaining three contemplations
Session 3	Meditation 6 – Developing renunciation, using all seven contemplations
Session 4	Meditation 6 – Developing renunciation, using all seven contemplations

DAY THREE

Session 1	Meditation 7 – Developing equanimity
Session 2	Meditation 8 – Recognizing that all living beings are our mothers
Session 3	Meditation 9 – Remembering the kindness of living beings
Session 4	Meditation 10 – Equalizing self and others

DAY FOUR

Session 1	Meditation 11 – The disadvantages of self-cherishing
Session 2	Meditation 12 – The advantages of cherishing others
Session 3	Meditation 13 – Exchanging self with others
Session 4	Meditation 14 – Great compassion

DAY FIVE

Session 1	Meditation 15 – Taking
Session 2	Meditation 16 – Wishing love
Session 3	Meditation 17 – Giving
Session 4	Meditation 18 – Bodhichitta

DAY SIX

All four sessions	Meditation 19 – Tranquil abiding, using either our chosen object or bodhichitta as our meditation object

DAY SEVEN

Session 1	Meditation 20 – Superior seeing, meditation on emptiness
Session 2	Meditation 20 – Superior seeing, meditation on emptiness
Session 3	Meditation 20 – Superior seeing, meditation on emptiness
Session 4	Meditation 21 – Relying upon a Spiritual Guide

Appendix V

The Commitments of Going for Refuge

The Commitments of Going for Refuge

When we go for refuge, we undertake to observe twelve special commitments. By observing these sincerely, we protect our mind of refuge and it gradually becomes more powerful. These commitments lay the foundation for all the realizations of the stages of the path. Realizing this, we should not regard them as a burden, but practise them joyfully and sincerely.

Within the twelve commitments, there are six specific commitments and six general commitments. The six specific commitments are so called because they are related specifically to each of the Three Jewels. There are two commitments related to Buddha, two related to Dharma, and two related to Sangha. In each case, there is one thing to abandon and one thing to practise. The remaining six commitments apply equally to Buddha, Dharma, and Sangha. These twelve commitments will now be briefly explained.

THE TWO COMMITMENTS SPECIFICALLY RELATED TO BUDDHA

1 Not to go for refuge to teachers who contradict Buddha's view, or to samsaric gods. By going for refuge to Buddha, we have a commitment to abandon going for ultimate refuge to teachers who contradict Buddha's view, or to worldly gods. This does not mean that we cannot receive help from others; it means that we do not rely upon others to provide ultimate protection from suffering.

2 To regard any image of Buddha as an actual Buddha. By going for refuge to Buddha, we also have a commitment to regard any image of Buddha as an actual Buddha. Whenever we see a statue of Buddha, whether it is made of gold or anything else, we should see it as an actual Buddha. We should disregard the material or the quality of the craftsmanship, and pay homage by making offerings and prostrations and by going for refuge. If we practise like this, our merit will increase abundantly.

THE TWO COMMITMENTS SPECIFICALLY RELATED TO DHARMA

3 Not to harm others. By going for refuge to Dharma, we have a commitment to abandon harming others. Instead of treating others badly, we should try, with the best motivation, to benefit them whenever we can. We first need to concentrate on reducing harmful thoughts and generating a beneficial intention towards those who are close to us, such as our friends and family. When we have developed a good heart towards these people, we can gradually extend our practice to include more and more people until, finally, we have a good heart towards all living beings. If we can abandon harmful thoughts and always have a beneficial intention, we shall easily attain the realizations of great love and great compassion. In this way, we begin to increase our compassion, which is the very essence of Buddhadharma, from the very beginning of our practice of going for refuge.

4 To regard all Dharma scriptures as the actual Dharma Jewel. By going for refuge to Dharma, we also have a commitment to regard all Dharma scriptures as the actual Dharma Jewel. Dharma is the source of all health and happiness. Since we cannot see actual Dharma Jewels with our eyes, we need to regard Dharma texts as actual Dharma Jewels. Actual Dharma Jewels arise only as a result of learning, contemplating, and meditating on the meaning of the scriptures. We need to respect every letter of the scriptures and every letter of explanation of Buddha's teaching. Therefore, we must treat Dharma books with great care and avoid walking over them or putting them in inappropriate places where they might be damaged or misused. Each time we neglect or spoil our Dharma books, we create the cause to become more ignorant because these actions are similar to the action of abandoning Dharma. Once the great Tibetan Teacher Geshe Sharawa saw some people playing carelessly with their Dharma books and he said to them, "You should not do that. You already have enough ignorance. Why do you want to make yourselves even more ignorant?"

THE TWO COMMITMENTS SPECIFICALLY RELATED TO SANGHA

5 Not to allow ourself to be influenced by people who reject Buddha's teaching. By going for refuge to Sangha, we have a commitment to stop being influenced by people who reject Buddha's teaching. This does not mean that we should abandon these people, merely that we should not let their views influence our mind. Without abandoning love and consideration for others, we need to be vigilant and make sure that we are not being led astray by their bad habits and unsound advice.

6 To regard anyone who wears the robes of an ordained person as an actual Sangha Jewel. By going for refuge to Sangha, we also have a commitment to acknowledge anyone who wears the robes of an ordained person as an actual Sangha Jewel. Even if ordained Sangha are poor, we still need to pay respect to them because they are keeping moral discipline and this is something very rare and precious.

THE SIX GENERAL COMMITMENTS

7 To go for refuge to the Three Jewels again and again, remembering their good qualities and the differences between them. Dharma is like a boat that can carry us across the ocean of samsara, Buddha is like the skilful navigator of the boat, and the Sangha are like the crew. Remembering this, we should go for refuge again and again to the Three Jewels.

8 To offer the first portion of whatever we eat and drink to the Three Jewels, while remembering their kindness. Since we need to eat and drink several times each day, if we always offer the first portion of our food or drink to the Three Jewels, remembering their kindness, we shall greatly increase our merit. We can do this with the following prayer:

I make this offering to you, Buddha Shakyamuni,
Whose mind is the synthesis of all Buddha Jewels,
Whose speech is the synthesis of all Dharma Jewels,
Whose body is the synthesis of all Sangha Jewels.
O Blessed One, please accept this and bless my mind.

OM AH HUM *(3x)*

It is important always to remember Buddha's kindness. All our happiness is a result of Buddha's kindness because all Buddha's actions are pervaded by compassion and concern for others, and it is these actions that enable us to perform virtuous actions that are the cause of our happiness.

Without Buddha's kindness, we would not know the real causes of happiness or the real causes of suffering. Buddha taught us how all happiness and suffering depend upon the mind. He showed us how to abandon those states of mind that cause suffering and cultivate those states of mind that cause happiness. In other words, he taught us perfect methods for overcoming suffering and attaining happiness. No one else taught us these methods. How kind Buddha is!

Our own human body is proof of Buddha's kindness. It is by virtue of Buddha's blessings and instructions that we were able to create the cause to take rebirth in a human form, with all the freedoms and endowments necessary for spiritual practice. If we are now able to learn Dharma and meet Spiritual Guides, it is only through Buddha's kindness. We can now practise the methods that lead to full enlightenment and gain spiritual realizations only because Buddha was kind enough to turn the Wheel of Dharma and show his example in this world. Even the small wisdom we possess to discriminate between what is beneficial and what is harmful, and to identify Buddha's teaching as worthwhile, is a result of Buddha's kindness.

We should not think that Buddha helps only those who follow him. Buddha attained enlightenment to benefit all living beings. He manifests in many different forms, sometimes even as non-Buddhist teachers, to help others. There is no living being who has not benefited from the kindness of Buddha.

9 With compassion, always to encourage others to go for refuge. We should always try to help others to go for refuge, but we should do so skilfully. If we know someone who is interested in Dharma, we should help him or her to develop the causes of going for refuge: fear of suffering and faith in the Three Jewels. We can talk to him or her about impermanence – how the conditions of this life change and how our body will grow old and decay – and we can talk about the sufferings of sickness, ageing, and death. We can talk about what will happen after death, about the different types of rebirth, and about how all types of rebirth are in the nature of suffering. If we skilfully introduce these things into our conversations, the other person will begin to lose his complacency and, when he starts to feel uneasy, he will naturally want to find out what can be done. At this point, we can explain about Buddha, Dharma, and Sangha, and how they can help us. Then we can explain how to go for refuge.

If we help someone else tactfully in this way, without being arrogant or impatient, we shall bring him or her real benefit. It is never certain that the material gifts we give to others will actually help them; sometimes they even cause more problems. The best way to help others is to lead them into Dharma. If we cannot give elaborate explanations, we can at least give appropriate advice to those who are unhappy, and help them to solve their problems by means of Dharma.

10 To go for refuge at least three times during the day and three times during the night, remembering the benefits of going for refuge. So that we never forget the Three Jewels, we should go for refuge once every four hours, or at least three times during the day and three times during the night. If we never forget the Three Jewels, and regularly contemplate the benefits of going for refuge, we shall gain realizations very quickly. We should be like a businessman who never forgets his projects even while he is relaxing.

11 To perform every action with complete trust in the Three Jewels. We should rely upon the Three Jewels in everything that we do. In this way, all our actions will be successful. There is no need to seek the inspiration and blessings of worldly gods, but we should always try to receive the blessings of Buddha, Dharma, and Sangha by making offerings and requests.

12 Never to forsake the Three Jewels, even at the cost of our life or as a joke. We should never abandon the Three Jewels, because going for refuge is the foundation of all Dharma realizations. Once a Buddhist was taken captive and his enemy said to him, "Give up your refuge in Buddha or I will kill you." He refused to forsake his refuge and was killed, but when clairvoyants looked, they saw that he had immediately been reborn as a god.

Appendix VI

A Traditional Meditation on Emptiness

A Traditional Meditation on Emptiness

FIRST CONTEMPLATION

The emptiness of the I

Identifying the object of negation

Although we grasp at an inherently existent I all the time, even during sleep, it is not easy to identify how it appears to our mind. To identify it clearly, we must begin by allowing it to manifest strongly by contemplating situations in which we have an exaggerated sense of I, such as when we are embarrassed, ashamed, afraid, or indignant. We recall or imagine such a situation and then, without any comment or analysis, try to attain a clear mental image of how the I naturally appears at such times. We have to be patient at this stage because it may take many sessions before we attain a clear image. Eventually we shall see that the I appears to be completely solid and real, existing from its own side without depending upon the body or the mind.

This vividly appearing I is the inherently existent I that we cherish so strongly. It is the I that we defend when we are criticized, and that we are so proud of when we are praised.

Once we have an image of how the I appears in these extreme circumstances, we should try to identify how it appears normally, in less extreme situations. For example, we can observe the I that is presently meditating and try to discover how it appears to our mind. Eventually we shall see that although in this case there is not such an inflated sense of I, nevertheless the I still appears to be inherently existent, existing from its own side without depending upon the body or the mind.

Once we have an image of the inherently existent I, we focus on it for a while with single-pointed concentration, and then we proceed to the second stage.

Refuting the object of negation

If the I exists in the way that it appears, it must exist in one of four ways: as the body, as the mind, as the collection of the body and mind, or as something separate from the body and mind; there is no other possibility. We contemplate this carefully until we become convinced that this is the case, and then we proceed to examine each of the four possibilities:

1 If the I is the body, there is no sense in saying, "my body", because the possessor and the possessed are identical.

  If the I is the body, there is no rebirth, because the I ceases when the body dies.

If the I and the body are identical, then, since we are capable of developing faith, dreaming, solving mathematical puzzles, and so on, it follows that flesh, blood, and bones can do the same.

Since none of this is true, it follows that the I is not the body.

2 If the I is the mind, there is no sense in saying, "my mind", because the possessor and the possessed are identical; but usually, when we focus on our mind, we say, "my mind". This clearly indicates that the I is not the mind.

If the I is the mind, then since each person has many types of mind, such as the six consciousnesses, conceptual minds, and non-conceptual minds, it follows that each person has just as many I's. Since this is absurd, it follows that the I is not the mind.

3 Since the body is not the I and the mind is not the I, the collection of the body and mind cannot be the I. The collection of the body and mind is a collection of things that are not the I, so how can the collection itself be the I? For example, in a herd of cows, none of the animals is a sheep, therefore the herd itself is not sheep. In the same way, in the collection of the body and mind, neither the body nor the mind is the I, therefore the collection itself is not the I.

You may find this point difficult to understand, but if you think about it for a long time with a calm and positive mind, and discuss it with more experienced practitioners, it will gradually become clear to you. You can also consult authentic books on the subject, such as *Heart of Wisdom*.

4 If the I is not the body, not the mind, and not the collection of the body and mind, the only possibility that remains is that it is something separate from the body and mind. If this is the case, we must be able to apprehend the I without either the body or the mind appearing, but, if we imagine that our body and our mind were completely to disappear, there would be nothing remaining that could be called the I. Therefore, it follows that the I is not separate from the body and mind.

We should imagine that our body gradually dissolves into thin air, and then our mind dissolves, our thoughts scatter with the wind, our feelings, wishes, and awareness melt into nothingness. Is there anything left that is the I? There is nothing. Clearly, the I is not something separate from the body and mind.

We have now examined all four possibilities and have failed to find the I. Since we have already decided that there is no fifth possibility, we must conclude that the truly existent, or inherently existent, I that normally appears so vividly does not exist at all. Where there previously appeared an inherently existent I, there now appears an absence of that I. This absence of an inherently existent I is emptiness, ultimate truth.

FIRST MEDITATION

We contemplate in this way until there appears to our mind a generic image of the absence of an inherently existent I. This image is our object of placement meditation. We try to become completely familiar with it by concentrating on it single-pointedly for as long as possible.

Because we have grasped at an inherently existent I since beginningless time, and have cherished it more dearly than anything else, the experience of failing to find the I in meditation can be quite shocking at first. Some people develop fear, thinking that they have become completely nonexistent. Others feel great joy, as if the source of all their problems is vanishing. Both reactions are good signs and indicate correct meditation. After a while, these initial reactions will subside and our mind will settle into a more balanced state. Then we shall be able to meditate on emptiness in a calm, controlled manner.

We should allow our mind to become absorbed in spacelike emptiness for as long as possible. It is important to remember that our object is emptiness, the absence of an inherently existent I, not mere nothingness. Occasionally we should check our meditation with alertness. If our mind has wandered to another object, or if we have lost the meaning of emptiness and are focusing on mere nothingness, we should return to the contemplations to bring emptiness clearly to mind once again.

We may wonder: "If there is no truly existent I, then who is meditating? Who will get up from meditation, speak to others, and reply when my name is called?" Though there is nothing within the body and mind, or separate from the body and mind, that is the I, this does not mean that the I does not exist at all. Although the I does not exist in any of the four ways mentioned above, it does exist conventionally. The I is merely a designation imputed by the conceptual mind upon the collection of the body and mind. So long as we are satisfied with the mere designation "I", there is no problem. We can think, "I exist", "I am going to town", and so on. The problem arises only when we look for an I other than the mere conceptual imputation "I". The self-grasping mind grasps at an I that ultimately exists, independent of conceptual imputation, as if there were a "real" I existing behind the label. If such an I existed, we would be able to find it, but we have seen that the I cannot be found upon investigation. The conclusion of our search was a definite non-finding of the I. This unfindability of the I is the emptiness of the I, the ultimate nature of the I. The I that exists as mere imputation is the conventional nature of the I.

SECOND CONTEMPLATION

The emptiness of the body

Identifying the object of negation

The way to meditate on the emptiness of the body is similar to the way we meditate on the emptiness of the I. First we must identify the object of negation.

Normally when we think, "my body", a body that exists from its own side and is a single entity not depending upon its parts, appears to our mind. Such a body is the object of negation and is non-existent. "Truly existent body", "inherently existent body", and "body that exists from its own side" all have the same meaning, and all are objects of negation.

Refuting the object of negation

If the body exists as it appears, it must exist in one of two ways: as its parts or separate from its parts; there is no third possibility.

If the body is one with its parts, is it the individual parts or the collection of its parts? If it is the individual parts, then is it the hands, the face, the skin, the bones, the flesh, or the internal organs? By checking carefully, "Is the head the body? Is the flesh the body?", and so on, we shall easily see that none of the individual parts of the body is the body.

If the body is not its individual parts, is it the collection of its parts? The collection of the parts of the body cannot be the body. Why? The parts of the body are all non-bodies, so how can a collection of non-bodies be a body? The hands, feet, and so forth are all parts of the body, but not the body itself. Even though all these parts are assembled together, this collection remains simply parts; it does not magically transform into the part-possessor, the body.

We should recall how our body appears to us when it is praised or insulted. It appears to be, from its own side, a distinct unit. It does not appear as something that is merely designated as a unit but which is in fact made up of many separate parts, like a forest or a herd of cows. Although the body appears as a single entity that exists from its own side without depending upon the limbs, trunk, and head, in reality it is merely designated to the collection of these parts. The collection of the parts of the body is an aggregation of many distinct elements that function together. This aggregation may be thought of as a unit, but that unit has no existence independent of its constituent parts.

If the body is not its parts, the only other possibility is that it is separate from its parts; but, if all the parts of the body were to disappear, there would be nothing left that could be called the body. We should imagine that all the parts of our body melt into light and disappear. First the skin dissolves, then the flesh, blood, and internal organs, and finally the skeleton melts and vanishes into light. Is there anything left that is our body? There is nothing. There is no body separate from its parts.

We have now exhausted all possibilities. The body is not its parts and it is not separate from its parts. Clearly, the body cannot be found. Where previously there appeared an inherently existent body, there now appears an absence of that body. This absence of an inherently existent body is the emptiness of the body.

SECOND MEDITATION

Recognizing this absence to be the lack of an inherently existent body, we meditate on it single-pointedly. Once again, we should examine our meditation with alertness to make sure that we are meditating on the emptiness of the body and not on nothingness. If we lose the meaning of emptiness, we should return to the contemplations to restore it.

As with the I, the fact that the body cannot be found upon investigation does not imply that the body does not exist at all. The body does exist, but only as a conventional imputation. In accordance with accepted convention, we can impute "body" to the assembly of limbs, trunk, and head; but if we try to pinpoint the body, hoping to find a substantially existent phenomenon to which the word "body" refers, we find no body. This unfindability of the body is the emptiness of the body, the ultimate nature of the body. The body that exists as mere imputation is the conventional nature of the body.

Although it is incorrect to assert that the body is identical with the collection of the limbs, trunk, and head, there is no fault in saying that the body is imputed upon this collection. Even though the parts of the body are plural, the body is singular. "Body" is simply an imputation made by the mind that imputes it. It does not exist from the object's side. There is no fault in imputing a singular phenomenon to a group of many things. For example, we can impute the singular "forest" to a group of many trees, or "herd" to a group of many cows.

All phenomena exist by way of convention; nothing is inherently existent. This applies to mind, Buddha, and even to emptiness itself. Everything is merely imputed by mind. All phenomena have parts because physical phenomena have physical parts and non-physical phenomena have various attributes that can be distinguished by thought. Using the same type of reasoning as above, we can realize that any phenomenon is not one of its parts, not the collection of its parts, and not separate from its parts. In this way, we can realize the emptiness of all phenomena.

It is particularly helpful to meditate on the emptiness of objects that arouse in us strong delusions such as attachment or anger. By analyzing correctly, we shall realize that the object we desire, or the object we dislike, does not exist from its own side – its beauty or ugliness, and even its very existence, are imputed by mind. By thinking in this way, we shall discover that there is no basis for attachment or anger.

Appendix VII

The Kadampa Way of Life

THE ESSENTIAL PRACTICE OF KADAM LAMRIM

Introduction

This essential practice of Kadam Lamrim, known as *The Kadampa Way of Life*, contains two texts: *Advice from Atisha's Heart* and Je Tsongkhapa's *The Three Principal Aspects of the Path*. The first encapsulates the way of life of the early Kadampa practitioners, whose example of purity and sincerity we should all try to emulate. The second is a profound guide to meditation on the stages of the path, Lamrim, which Je Tsongkhapa composed based on the instructions he received directly from the Wisdom Buddha Manjushri.

If we try our best to put Atisha's advice into practice, and to meditate on Lamrim according to Je Tsongkhapa's instructions, we shall develop a pure and happy mind and gradually progress towards the ultimate peace of full enlightenment. As Bodhisattva Shantideva says:

By depending upon this boat-like human form,
We can cross the great ocean of suffering.
Since such a vessel will be hard to find again,
This is no time to sleep, you fool!

Practising in this way is the very essence of the Kadampa way of life.

Advice from Atisha's Heart

When Venerable Atisha came to Tibet, he first went to Ngari, where he remained for two years giving many teachings to the disciples of Jangchub Ö. After two years had passed, he decided to return to India, and Jangchub Ö requested him to give one last teaching before he left. Atisha replied that he had already given them all the advice they needed, but Jangchub Ö persisted in his request and so Atisha accepted and gave the following advice.

How wonderful!

Friends, since you already have great knowledge and clear understanding, whereas I am of no importance and have little wisdom, it is not suitable for you to request advice from me. However because you dear friends, whom I cherish from my heart, have requested me, I shall give you this essential advice from my inferior and childish mind.

Friends, until you attain enlightenment the Spiritual Teacher is indispensable, therefore rely upon the holy Spiritual Guide.

Until you realize ultimate truth, listening is indispensable, therefore listen to the instructions of the Spiritual Guide.

Since you cannot become a Buddha merely by understanding Dharma, practise earnestly with understanding.

Avoid places that disturb your mind, and always remain where your virtues increase.

Until you attain stable realizations, worldly amusements are harmful, therefore abide in a place where there are no such distractions.

Avoid friends who cause you to increase delusions, and rely upon those who increase your virtue. This you should take to heart.

Since there is never a time when worldly activities come to an end, limit your activities.

Dedicate your virtues throughout the day and the night, and always watch your mind.

Because you have received advice, whenever you are not meditating, always practise in accordance with what your Spiritual Guide says.

If you practise with great devotion, results will arise immediately, without your having to wait for a long time.

If from your heart you practise in accordance with Dharma, both food and resources will come naturally to hand.

Friends, the things you desire give no more satisfaction than drinking sea water, therefore practise contentment.

Avoid all haughty, conceited, proud, and arrogant minds, and remain peaceful and subdued.

Avoid activities that are said to be meritorious, but which in fact are obstacles to Dharma.

Profit and respect are nooses of the maras, so brush them aside like stones on the path.

Words of praise and fame serve only to beguile us, therefore blow them away as you would blow your nose.

Since the happiness, pleasure, and friends you gather in this life last only for a moment, put them all behind you.

Since future lives last for a very long time, gather up riches to provide for the future.

You will have to depart leaving everything behind, so do not be attached to anything.

Generate compassion for lowly beings, and especially avoid despising or humiliating them.

Have no hatred for enemies, and no attachment for friends.

Do not be jealous of others' good qualities, but out of admiration adopt them yourself.

Do not look for faults in others, but look for faults in yourself, and purge them like bad blood.

Do not contemplate your own good qualities, but contemplate the good qualities of others, and respect everyone as a servant would.

See all living beings as your father or mother, and love them as if you were their child.

Always keep a smiling face and a loving mind, and speak truthfully without malice.

If you talk too much with little meaning, you will make mistakes, therefore speak in moderation, only when necessary.

If you engage in many meaningless activities, your virtuous activities will degenerate, therefore stop activities that are not spiritual.

It is completely meaningless to put effort into activities that have no essence.

If the things you desire do not come, it is due to karma created long ago, therefore keep a happy and relaxed mind.

Beware, offending a holy being is worse than dying, therefore be honest and straightforward.

Since all the happiness and suffering of this life arise from previous actions, do not blame others.

All happiness comes from the blessings of your Spiritual Guide, therefore always repay his kindness.

Since you cannot tame the minds of others until you have tamed your own, begin by taming your own mind.

Since you will definitely have to depart without the wealth you have accumulated, do not accumulate negativity for the sake of wealth.

Distracting enjoyments have no essence, therefore sincerely practise giving.

Always keep pure moral discipline for it leads to beauty in this life and happiness hereafter.

Since hatred is rife in these impure times, don the armour of patience, free from anger.

You remain in samsara through the power of laziness, therefore ignite the fire of the effort of application.

Since this human life is wasted by indulging in distractions, now is the time to practise concentration.

Being under the influence of wrong views, you do not realize the ultimate nature of things, therefore investigate correct meanings.

Friends, there is no happiness in this swamp of samsara, so move to the firm ground of liberation.

Meditate according to the advice of your Spiritual Guide and dry up the river of samsaric suffering.

You should consider this well because it is not just words from the mouth, but sincere advice from the heart.

If you practise like this, you will delight me, and you will bring happiness to yourself and others.

I who am ignorant request you to take this advice to heart.

This is the advice that the holy being Venerable Atisha gave to Venerable Jangchub Ö.

The Three Principal Aspects of the Path

Homage to the venerable Spiritual Guide.

I shall explain to the best of my ability
The essential meaning of all the Conqueror's teachings,
The path praised by the holy Bodhisattvas,
And the gateway for fortunate ones seeking liberation.

You who are not attached to the joys of samsara,
But strive to make your freedom and endowment meaningful,
O Fortunate Ones who apply your minds to the path that pleases the Conquerors,
Please listen with a clear mind.

Without pure renunciation, there is no way to pacify
Attachment to the pleasures of samsara;
And since living beings are tightly bound by desire for samsara,
Begin by seeking renunciation.

Freedom and endowment are difficult to find, and there
is no time to waste.
By acquainting your mind with this, overcome
attachment to this life;
And by repeatedly contemplating actions and effects
And the sufferings of samsara, overcome attachment to
future lives.

When, through contemplating in this way, the desire for
the pleasures of samsara
Does not arise, even for a moment,
But a mind longing for liberation arises throughout the
day and the night,
At that time, renunciation is generated.

However, if this renunciation is not maintained
By completely pure bodhichitta,
It will not be a cause of the perfect happiness of
unsurpassed enlightenment;
Therefore, the wise generate a supreme bodhichitta.

Swept along by the currents of the four powerful rivers,
Tightly bound by the chains of karma, so hard to release,
Ensnared within the iron net of self-grasping,
Completely enveloped by the pitch-black darkness of
ignorance,

Taking rebirth after rebirth in boundless samsara,
And unceasingly tormented by the three sufferings –
Through contemplating the state of your mothers in
conditions such as these,
Generate a supreme mind [of bodhichitta].

But, even though you may be acquainted with
renunciation and bodhichitta,
If you do not possess the wisdom realizing the way
things are,
You will not be able to cut the root of samsara;
Therefore, strive in the means for realizing dependent
relationship.

Whoever negates the conceived object of self-grasping
Yet sees the infallibility of cause and effect
Of all phenomena in samsara and nirvana,
Has entered the path that pleases the Buddhas.

Dependent-related appearance is infallible
And emptiness is inexpressible;
For as long as the meaning of these two appear to be
separate,
You have not yet realized Buddha's intention.

When they arise as one, not alternating but simultaneous,
From merely seeing infallible dependent relationship
Comes certain knowledge that destroys all grasping at
objects.
At that time, the analysis of view is complete.

Moreover, when the extreme of existence is dispelled by
appearance,
And the extreme of non-existence is dispelled by
emptiness,
And you know how emptiness is perceived as cause and
effect,
You will not be captivated by extreme views.

When, in this way, you have correctly realized the
essential points
Of the three principal aspects of the path,
Dear One, withdraw into solitude, generate strong effort,
And quickly accomplish the final goal.

Colophon: Both texts were translated under the compassionate guidance of Geshe Kelsang Gyatso Rinpoche.

Glossary

Alertness A mental factor which is a type of wisdom that examines our activity of body, speech, and mind and knows whether or not faults are developing. See *Understanding the Mind*.

Anger A deluded mental factor that observes its contaminated object, exaggerates its bad qualities, considers it to be undesirable, and wishes to harm it. See *Understanding the Mind*.

Atisha (AD 982-1054) A famous Indian Buddhist scholar and meditation master. He was Abbot of the great Buddhist monastery of Vikramashila at a time when Mahayana Buddhism was flourishing in India. He was later invited to Tibet and his arrival there led to the re-establishment of Buddhism in Tibet. He is the author of the first text on the stages of the path, *Lamp for the Path*. His tradition later became known as the "Kadampa Tradition". See *Joyful Path of Good Fortune*.

Attachment A deluded mental factor that observes a contaminated object, regards it as a cause of happiness, and wishes for it. See *Understanding the Mind*.

Beginningless time According to the Buddhist world view, there is no beginning to mind, and so no beginning to time. Therefore, all living beings have taken countless previous rebirths.

Blessing "Jin gyi lab pa" in Tibetan. The transformation of our mind from a negative state to a positive state, from an unhappy state to a happy state, or from a state of weakness to a state of strength, through the inspiration of holy beings such as our Spiritual Guide, Buddhas, and Bodhisattvas.

Bodhichitta Sanskrit word for "mind of enlightenment". "Bodhi" means "enlightenment", and "chitta" means "mind". There are two types of bodhichitta – conventional bodhichitta and ultimate bodhichitta. Generally speaking, the term "bodhichitta" refers to conventional bodhichitta, which is the mind that spontaneously wishes to attain enlightenment for the benefit of all living beings. There are two types of conventional bodhichitta – aspiring bodhichitta and engaging bodhichitta. Aspiring bodhichitta is a bodhichitta that is a mere wish to attain enlightenment for the benefit of all living beings. Engaging bodhichitta is a bodhichitta held by the Bodhisattva vows. Ultimate bodhichitta is a wisdom motivated by conventional bodhichitta that directly realizes emptiness, the ultimate nature of phenomena. In general, there are two methods for developing conventional bodhichitta: the method of the sevenfold cause and effect, and the method of equalizing and exchanging self with others. The system presented in *The New Meditation Handbook* is a synthesis of these two traditions. See also *Sevenfold cause and effect*. See *Joyful Path of Good Fortune* and *Meaningful to Behold*.

Bodhisattva A person who has generated spontaneous bodhichitta but who has not yet become a Buddha. From the moment a practitioner generates a non-artificial, or spontaneous, bodhichitta, he or she becomes a Bodhisattva and enters the first Mahayana path, the path of accumulation. An ordinary Bodhisattva is one who has not realized emptiness directly, and a Superior Bodhisattva is one who has attained a direct realization of emptiness. See *Joyful Path of Good Fortune* and *Meaningful to Behold.*

Bodhisattva vow See *Vow.*

Buddha In general, "Buddha" means "Awakened One", someone who has awakened from the sleep of ignorance and sees things as they really are. A Buddha is a person who is completely free from all faults and mental obstructions. Every living being has the potential to become a Buddha.

Buddhadharma See *Dharma.*

Buddhahood Synonymous with full enlightenment. See *Enlightenment.*

Buddha seed The root mind of a sentient being, and its ultimate nature. Buddha seed, Buddha nature, and Buddha lineage are synonyms. All sentient beings have Buddha seed and therefore the potential to attain Buddhahood.

Buddha Shakyamuni The Buddha who is the founder of the Buddhist religion. See *Introduction to Buddhism.*

Buddhist Anyone who from the depths of his or her heart goes for refuge to the Three Jewels – Buddha Jewel, Dharma Jewel, and Sangha Jewel. See *Introduction to Buddhism.*

Changing suffering For samsaric beings, every experience of happiness or pleasure that arises from samsara's enjoyments is changing suffering, because these experiences are contaminated and have the nature of suffering. See *Joyful Path of Good Fortune.*

Clairvoyance Abilities that arise from special concentration. There are five principal types of clairvoyance: the clairvoyance of divine eye (the ability to see subtle and distant forms), the clairvoyance of divine ear (the ability to hear subtle and distant sounds), the clairvoyance of miracle powers (the ability to emanate various forms by mind), the clairvoyance of knowing previous lives, and the clairvoyance of knowing others' minds. Some beings, such as bardo beings and some human beings and spirits, have contaminated clairvoyance that is developed due to karma, but these are not actual clairvoyance.

Clear light A manifest very subtle mind that perceives an appearance like clear, empty space. See *Clear Light of Bliss* and *Tantric Grounds and Paths*.

Completion stage Highest Yoga Tantra realizations developed in dependence upon the winds entering, abiding, and dissolving within the central channel through the force of meditation. See *Clear Light of Bliss* and *Tantric Grounds and Paths*.

Concentration A mental factor that makes its primary mind remain on its object single-pointedly. See *Joyful Path of Good Fortune* and *Understanding the Mind*.

Conceptual mind A thought that apprehends its object through a generic, or mental, image. See *Understanding the Mind*.

Confession Purification of negative karma by means of the four opponent powers – the power of reliance, the power of regret, the power of the opponent force, and the power of promise. See *The Bodhisattva Vow* and *Universal Compassion*.

Conscientiousness A mental factor that, in dependence upon effort, cherishes what is virtuous and guards the mind from delusion and non-virtue. See *Meaningful to Behold*.

Consciousness The six consciousnesses, or six primary minds, are the eye consciousness, ear consciousness, nose consciousness, tongue consciousness, body consciousness, and mental consciousness. See *Understanding the Mind*.

Contentment Being satisfied with one's inner and outer conditions, motivated by a virtuous intention.

Dedication Dedication is by nature a virtuous mental factor; it is the virtuous intention that functions both to prevent accumulated virtue from degenerating and to cause its increase. See *Joyful Path of Good Fortune.*

Delusion A mental factor that arises from inappropriate attention and functions to make the mind unpeaceful and uncontrolled. There are three main delusions: ignorance, desirous attachment, and anger. From these arise all the other delusions, such as jealousy, pride, and deluded doubt. See *Joyful Path of Good Fortune.*

Desire realm The environment of hell beings, hungry spirits, animals, human beings, demi-gods, and the gods who enjoy the five objects of desire.

Dharma Buddha's teachings and the inner realizations that are attained in dependence upon practising them. "Dharma" means "protection". By practising Buddha's teachings, we protect ourself from suffering and problems.

Emptiness Lack of inherent existence, the ultimate nature of phenomena. See *Heart of Wisdom.*

Energy winds See *Inner winds.*

Enlightenment Omniscient wisdom free from all mistaken appearances. See *Transform Your Life* and *Joyful Path of Good Fortune.*

Faith A naturally virtuous mind that functions mainly to oppose the perception of faults in its observed object. There are three types of faith: believing faith, admiring faith, and wishing faith. See *Transform Your Life.*

Form realm The environment of the gods who possess form.

Formless realm The environment of the gods who do not possess form.

Generic image The appearing object of a conceptual mind. A generic image, or mental image, of an object is like a reflection of that object. Conceptual minds know their object through the appearance of a generic image of that object, not by seeing the object directly. See *Understanding the Mind.*

Geshe A title given by Kadampa monasteries to accomplished Buddhist scholars. Contracted form of the Tibetan "ge wai she nyen", literally meaning "virtuous friend".

Guru See *Spiritual Guide.*

Happiness There are two types of happiness: mundane and supramundane. Mundane happiness is the limited happiness that can be found within samsara, such as the happiness of human beings and gods. Supramundane happiness is the pure happiness of liberation and enlightenment.

Heart channel wheel The channel wheel (Skt. chakra) at our heart. Sometimes known as "spiritual heart". See *Clear Light of Bliss* and *Tantric Grounds and Paths.*

Highest Yoga Tantra A Tantric instruction that includes the method for transforming sexual bliss into the spiritual path. See *Tantric Grounds and Paths.*

Imprint There are two types of imprint: imprints of actions and imprints of delusions. Every action we perform leaves an imprint on the mental consciousness, and these imprints are karmic potentialities to experience certain effects in the future. The imprints left by delusions remain even after the delusions themselves have been abandoned, rather as the smell of garlic lingers in a container after the garlic has been removed. Imprints of delusions are obstructions to omniscience, and are completely abandoned only by Buddhas.

Imputation, mere According to the highest school of Buddhist philosophy, the Madhyamika-Prasangika school, all phenomena are merely imputed by conception in dependence upon their basis of imputation. Therefore, they are mere imputation and do not exist from their own side in the least. See *Heart of Wisdom*.

Inner winds Special subtle winds related to the mind that flow through the channels of our body. Our body and mind cannot function without these winds. See *Clear Light of Bliss* and *Tantric Grounds and Paths*.

Je Tsongkhapa (AD 1357-1419) An emanation of the Wisdom Buddha Manjushri, whose appearance in fourteenth-century Tibet as a monk, and the holder of the lineage of pure view and pure deeds, was prophesied by Buddha. He spread a very pure Buddhadharma throughout Tibet, showing how to combine the practices of Sutra and Tantra, and how to practise pure Dharma during degenerate times. His tradition later became known as the "Gelug", or "Ganden Tradition". See *Heart Jewel* and *Great Treasury of Merit*.

Kadampa A Tibetan word in which "Ka" means "word" and refers to all Buddha's teachings, "dam" refers to Atisha's special Lamrim instructions known as the "stages of the path to enlightenment", and "pa" refers to a follower of Kadampa Buddhism who integrates all the teachings of Buddha that they know into their Lamrim practice. See also *Kadampa Buddhism* and *Kadampa Tradition*.

Kadampa Buddhism A Mahayana Buddhist school founded by the great Indian Buddhist Master Atisha (AD 982-1054). See also *Kadampa* and *Kadampa Tradition*.

Kadampa Tradition The pure tradition of Buddhism established by Atisha. Followers of this tradition up to the time of Je Tsongkhapa are known as "Old Kadampas", and those after the time of Je Tsongkhapa are known as "New Kadampas". See also *Kadampa* and *Kadampa Buddhism*.

Karma Sanskrit word meaning "action". Through the force of intention, we perform actions with our body, speech, and mind, and all of these actions produce effects. The effect of virtuous actions is happiness and the effect of negative actions is suffering. See *Joyful Path of Good Fortune.*

Lamrim A Tibetan term, literally meaning "stages of the path". A special arrangement of all Buddha's teachings that is easy to understand and put into practice. It reveals all the stages of the path to enlightenment. For a full commentary, see *Joyful Path of Good Fortune.*

Life-supporting wind An inner energy wind that resides in the heart chakra. This wind has three levels: gross, subtle, and very subtle. It is the very subtle wind that travels from life to life, supporting the very subtle mind. See *Clear Light of Bliss.*

Living being (Tib. sem chän) Any being who possesses a mind that is contaminated by delusions or their imprints. Both "living being" and "sentient being" are terms used to distinguish beings whose minds are contaminated by either of these two obstructions from Buddhas, whose minds are completely free from these obstructions.

Mahayana Sanskrit word for "Great Vehicle", the spiritual path to great enlightenment. The Mahayana goal is to attain Buddhahood for the benefit of all sentient beings by completely abandoning delusions and their imprints. See *Joyful Path of Good Fortune.*

Manjushri The embodiment of the wisdom of all the Buddhas. See *Great Treasury of Merit* and *Heart Jewel.*

Mantra A Sanskrit word, literally meaning "mind protection". Mantra protects the mind from ordinary appearances and conceptions. There are four types of mantra: mantras that are mind, mantras that are inner wind, mantras that are sound, and mantras that are form. In general, there are three types of mantra recitation: verbal recitation, mental recitation, and vajra recitation. See *Tantric Grounds and Paths.*

Mental image See *Generic image.*

Merit The good fortune created by virtuous actions. It is the potential power to increase our good qualities and produce happiness.

Milarepa (AD 1040-1123) A great Tibetan Buddhist meditator and disciple of Marpa, celebrated for his beautiful songs of realization.

Mind That which is clarity and cognizes. Mind is clarity because it always lacks form and because it possesses the actual power to perceive objects. Mind cognizes because its function is to know or perceive objects. See *Understanding the Mind.*

Mindfulness A mental factor that functions not to forget the object realized by the primary mind. See *Understanding the Mind.*

Miracle powers See *Clairvoyance.*

Moral discipline A virtuous mental determination to abandon any fault, or a bodily or verbal action motivated by such a determination. See *Joyful Path of Good Fortune.*

Mount Meru According to Buddhist cosmology, a divine mountain that stands at the centre of the universe.

New Kadampa Tradition See *Kadampa Tradition.*

Nine mental abidings Nine levels of concentration leading to tranquil abiding: placing the mind, continual placement, replacement, close placement, controlling, pacifying, completely pacifying, single-pointedness, and placement in equipoise. See *Joyful Path of Good Fortune* and *Meaningful to Behold.*

Non-conceptual mind A cognizer to which its object appears clearly without being mixed with a generic image. See *Understanding the Mind.*

Non-virtuous actions Paths that lead to the lower realms. Non-virtuous actions are countless, but most of them are included within the ten: killing, stealing, sexual misconduct, lying, divisive speech, hurtful speech, idle gossip, covetousness, malice, and holding wrong views. See *Joyful Path of Good Fortune.*

Pratimoksha Sanskrit word for "individual liberation". See *The Bodhisattva Vow.*

Pure Land A pure environment in which there are no true sufferings. There are many Pure Lands. For example, Tushita is the Pure Land of Buddha Maitreya; Sukhavati is the Pure Land of Buddha Amitabha; and Dakini Land, or Keajra, is the Pure Land of Buddha Vajrayogini and Buddha Heruka. See *Living Meaningfully, Dying Joyfully.*

Purification Generally, any practice that leads to the attainment of a pure body, speech, or mind. More specifically, a practice for purifying negative karma by means of the four opponent powers. See *The Bodhisattva Vow.*

Realization A stable and non-mistaken experience of a virtuous object that directly protects us from suffering.

Retreat A period of time during which we impose various restrictions on our actions of body, speech, and mind so as to be able to concentrate more fully on a particular spiritual practice. See *Heart Jewel.*

Sangha According to the Vinaya tradition, any community of four or more fully ordained monks or nuns. In general, ordained or lay people who take Bodhisattva vows or Tantric vows can also be said to be Sangha.

Self-grasping A conceptual mind that holds any phenomenon to be inherently existent. The mind of self-grasping gives rise to all other delusions, such as anger and attachment. It is the root cause of all suffering and dissatisfaction. See *Heart of Wisdom*.

Sentient being See *Living being*.

Sevenfold cause and effect A method for generating bodhichitta in which affectionate love is developed primarily by recognizing all sentient beings as our mothers and remembering their kindness. See *Joyful Path of Good Fortune*.

Shantideva (AD 687-763) A great Indian Buddhist scholar and meditation master. He composed *Guide to the Bodhisattva's Way of Life*. See *Meaningful to Behold*.

Spiritual Guide "Guru" in Sanskrit, "Lama" in Tibetan. A Teacher who guides us along the spiritual path. See *Joyful Path of Good Fortune*.

Stages of the path See *Lamrim*.

Superior being "Arya" in Sanskrit. A being who has a direct realization of emptiness. There are Hinayana Superiors and Mahayana Superiors.

Superior intention The determination to take personal responsibility to release others from suffering and lead them to perfect happiness. See *Joyful Path of Good Fortune*.

Suppleness There are two types of suppleness, mental and physical. Mental suppleness is a flexibility of mind induced by virtuous concentration. Physical suppleness is a light and flexible tactile object within our body that develops when meditation causes a pure wind to pervade the body.

Sutra The teachings of Buddha that are open to everyone to practise without the need for empowerment. These include Buddha's teachings of the three turnings of the Wheel of Dharma.

Tantra Tantric teachings are distinguished from Sutra teachings in that they reveal methods for training the mind by bringing the future result, or Buddhahood, into the present path. Tantric practitioners overcome ordinary appearances and conceptions by visualizing their body, environment, enjoyments, and deeds as those of a Buddha. Tantra is the supreme path to full enlightenment. Tantric practices are to be done in private and only by those who have received a Tantric empowerment. Synonymous with "Secret Mantra". See *Tantric Grounds and Paths*.

Three higher trainings Training in moral discipline, concentration, and wisdom motivated by renunciation or bodhichitta.

Three Jewels The three objects of refuge: Buddha Jewel, Dharma Jewel, and Sangha Jewel. They are called "Jewels" because they are both rare and precious. See *Joyful Path of Good Fortune*.

Three principal aspects of the path The realizations of renunciation, bodhichitta, and wisdom realizing emptiness. See *Joyful Path of Good Fortune*.

Vajra Generally, the Sanskrit word "vajra" means indestructible like a diamond and powerful like a thunderbolt. In the context of Tantra, it can mean the indivisibility of method and wisdom, omniscient great wisdom, or spontaneous great bliss. It is also the name given to a metal ritual object. See *Tantric Grounds and Paths*.

Vajradhara The founder of Vajrayana, or Tantra. He is the same mental continuum as Buddha Shakyamuni but displays a different aspect. Buddha Shakyamuni appears in the aspect of an Emanation Body, and Conqueror Vajradhara appears in the aspect of an Enjoyment Body. See *Great Treasury of Merit*.

Vajra posture A perfect posture for meditation, in which the legs are crossed in the full vajra posture, with the left foot placed sole upwards on the right thigh and the right foot sole upwards on the left thigh. The right hand is placed on top of the left hand with both palms facing upwards, and the two thumbs are raised and touching at the level of the navel. The back is straight and the shoulders are level. The mouth is gently closed, the head is inclined very slightly forwards, and the eyes are neither wide open nor tightly closed but either slightly open or gently closed. See *Joyful Path of Good Fortune.*

Vow A virtuous determination to abandon particular faults that is generated in conjunction with a traditional ritual. The three sets of vows are the Pratimoksha vows of individual liberation, the Bodhisattva vows, and the Tantric vows. See *The Bodhisattva Vow* and *Tantric Grounds and Paths.*

Wheel of Dharma Buddha gave his teachings in three main phases, which are known as "the three turnings of the Wheel of Dharma". During the first Wheel he taught the four noble truths, during the second he taught the *Perfection of Wisdom Sutras* and revealed the Madhyamika-Prasangika view, and during the third he taught the Chittâmatra view. These teachings were given according to the inclinations and dispositions of his disciples. Buddha's final view is that of the second Wheel. Dharma is compared to the precious wheel, one of the possessions of a legendary chakravatin king. This wheel could transport the king across great distances in a very short time, and it is said that wherever the precious wheel travelled the king reigned. In a similar way, when Buddha revealed the path to enlightenment he was said to have "turned the Wheel of Dharma" because wherever these teachings are present deluded minds are brought under control.

Wishfulfilling jewel A legendary jewel that, like Aladdin's lamp, grants whatever is wished for.

Bibliography

Geshe Kelsang Gyatso is a highly respected meditation master and scholar of the Mahayana Buddhist tradition founded by Je Tsongkhapa. Since arriving in the West in 1977, Geshe Kelsang has worked tirelessly to establish pure Buddhadharma throughout the world. Over this period he has given extensive teachings on the major scriptures of the Mahayana. These teachings are currently being published and provide a comprehensive presentation of the essential Sutra and Tantra practices of Mahayana Buddhism.

Books

The following books by Geshe Kelsang are all published by Tharpa Publications.

The Bodhisattva Vow. A practical guide to helping others. (2nd. edn., 1995)

Clear Light of Bliss. Tantric meditation manual. (2nd. edn., 1992)

Eight Steps to Happiness. The Buddhist way of loving kindness. (2000)

Essence of Vajrayana. The Highest Yoga Tantra practice of Heruka body mandala. (1997)

Great Treasury of Merit. The practice of relying upon a Spiritual Guide. (1992)

Guide to Dakini Land. The Highest Yoga Tantra practice of Buddha Vajrayogini. (2nd. edn., 1996)

Guide to the Bodhisattva's Way of Life. How to enjoy a life of great meaning and altruism. (A translation of Shantideva's famous verse masterpiece.) (2002)

Heart Jewel. The essential practices of Kadampa Buddhism. (2nd. edn., 1997)

Heart of Wisdom. An explanation of the *Heart Sutra.* (4th. edn., 2001)

Introduction to Buddhism. An explanation of the Buddhist way of life. (2nd. edn., 2001)

Joyful Path of Good Fortune. The complete Buddhist path to enlightenment. (2nd. edn., 1995)

Living Meaningfully, Dying Joyfully. The profound practice of transference of consciousness. (1999)

Meaningful to Behold. The Bodhisattva's way of life. (4th. edn., 1994)

The New Meditation Handbook. Meditations to make our life happy and meaningful. (2003)

Ocean of Nectar. The true nature of all things. (1995)

Tantric Grounds and Paths. How to enter, progress on, and complete the Vajrayana path. (1994)

Transform Your Life. A blissful journey. (2001)

Understanding the Mind. The nature and power of the mind. (2nd. edn., 1997)

Universal Compassion. Inspiring solutions for difficult times (4th. edn., 2002)

Sadhanas

Geshe Kelsang has also supervised the translation of a collection of essential sadhanas, or prayer booklets.

Assembly of Good Fortune. The tsog offering for Heruka body mandala.

Avalokiteshvara Sadhana. Prayers and requests to the Buddha of Compassion.

The Bodhisattva's Confession of Moral Downfalls. The purification practice of the *Mahayana Sutra of the Three Superior Heaps*.

Condensed Essence of Vajrayana. Condensed Heruka body mandala self-generation sadhana.

Dakini Yoga. Six-session Guru yoga combined with self-generation as Vajrayogini.

Drop of Essential Nectar. A special fasting and purification practice in conjunction with Eleven-faced Avalokiteshvara.

Essence of Good Fortune. Prayers for the six preparatory practices for meditation on the stages of the path to enlightenment.

Essence of Vajrayana. Heruka body mandala self-generation sadhana according to the system of Mahasiddha Ghantapa.

Feast of Great Bliss. Vajrayogini self-initiation sadhana.

Great Compassionate Mother. The sadhana of Arya Tara.

Great Liberation of the Mother. Preliminary prayers for Mahamudra meditation in conjunction with Vajrayogini practice.

The Great Mother. A method to overcome hindrances and obstacles by reciting the *Essence of Wisdom Sutra* (the *Heart Sutra*).

Heartfelt Prayers. Funeral service for cremations and burials.

Heart Jewel. The Guru yoga of Je Tsongkhapa combined with the condensed sadhana of his Dharma Protector.

The Hundreds of Deities of the Joyful Land. The Guru yoga of Je Tsongkhapa.

The Kadampa Way of Life. The essential practice of Kadam Lamrim.
Liberation from Sorrow. Praises and requests to the Twenty-one Taras.
Mahayana Refuge Ceremony and Bodhisattva Vow Ceremony.
Medicine Buddha Sadhana. The method for making requests to the Assembly of Seven Medicine Buddhas.
Meditation and Recitation of Solitary Vajrasattva.
Melodious Drum Victorious in all Directions. The extensive fulfilling and restoring ritual of the Dharma Protector, the great king Dorje Shugdän, in conjunction with Mahakala, Kalarupa, Kalindewi, and other Dharma Protectors.
Offering to the Spiritual Guide (*Lama Chöpa*). A special Guru yoga practice of Je Tsongkhapa's tradition.
Pathway to the Pure Land. Training in powa – the transference of consciousness.
Prayers for Meditation. Brief preparatory prayers for meditation.
A Pure Life. The practice of taking and keeping the eight Mahayana precepts.
The Quick Path. A condensed practice of Heruka Five Deities according to Master Ghantapa's tradition.
Quick Path to Great Bliss. Vajrayogini self-generation sadhana.
Treasury of Blessings. The condensed meaning of Vajrayana Mahamudra and prayers of request to the lineage Gurus.
Treasury of Wisdom. The sadhana of Venerable Manjushri.
Vajra Hero Yoga. A brief essential practice of Heruka body mandala self-generation, and condensed six-session yoga.
The Vows and Commitments of Kadampa Buddhism.
Wishfulfilling Jewel. The Guru yoga of Je Tsongkhapa combined with the sadhana of his Dharma Protector.
The Yoga of Buddha Amitayus. A special method for increasing lifespan, wisdom, and merit.
The Yoga of White Tara, Buddha of Long Life.

To order any of our publications, or to receive a catalogue, please contact:

Tharpa Publications
Conishead Priory
Ulverston
Cumbria, LA12 9QQ
England

Tel: 01229-588599
Fax: 01229-483919

E-mail: tharpa@tharpa.com
Website: www.tharpa.com

or

Tharpa Publications
47 Sweeney Road
P.O. Box 430
Glen Spey, NY 12737
USA

Tel: 845-856-5102 or
888-741-3475 (toll free)
Fax: 845-856-2110

Email: tharpa-us@tharpa.com
Website: www.tharpa.com

Study Programmes of Kadampa Buddhism

Kadampa Buddhism is a Mahayana Buddhist school founded by the great Indian Buddhist Master Atisha (AD 982-1054). His followers are known as "Kadampas". "Ka" means "word" and refers to Buddha's teachings, and "dam" refers to Atisha's special Lamrim instructions known as "the stages of the path to enlightenment". By integrating their knowledge of all Buddha's teachings into their practice of Lamrim, and by integrating this into their everyday lives, Kadampa Buddhists are encouraged to use Buddha's teachings as practical methods for transforming daily activities into the path to enlightenment. The great Kadampa Teachers are famous not only for being great scholars, but also for being spiritual practitioners of immense purity and sincerity.

The lineage of these teachings, both their oral transmission and blessings, was then passed from Teacher to disciple, spreading throughout much of Asia, and now to many countries throughout the Western world. Buddha's teachings, which are known as "Dharma", are likened to a wheel that moves from country to country in accordance with changing conditions and people's karmic inclinations. The external forms of presenting Buddhism may change as it meets with different cultures and societies, but its essential authenticity is ensured through the continuation of an unbroken lineage of realized practitioners.

Kadampa Buddhism was first introduced into the West in 1977 by the renowned Buddhist Master, Venerable Geshe Kelsang Gyatso. Since that time, he has worked tirelessly to spread Kadampa Buddhism throughout the world by giving extensive teachings, writing many profound texts on Kadampa Buddhism, and founding the New Kadampa Tradition (NKT), which now has over four hundred Kadampa Buddhist Centres worldwide. Each Centre offers study programmes on Buddhist psychology, philosophy, and meditation instruction, as well as retreats for all levels of practitioner. The emphasis is on integrating Buddha's teachings into daily life to solve our human problems and to spread lasting peace and happiness throughout the world.

The Kadampa Buddhism of the NKT is an entirely independent Buddhist tradition and has no political affiliations. It is an association of Buddhist Centres and practitioners that derive their inspiration and guidance from the example of the ancient Kadampa Buddhist Masters and their teachings, as presented by Geshe Kelsang.

There are three reasons why we need to study and practise the teachings of Buddha: to develop our wisdom, to cultivate a good heart, and to maintain a peaceful state of mind. If we do not strive to develop our wisdom, we will always remain ignorant of ultimate truth – the true nature of reality. Although we wish for happiness, our ignorance leads us to engage in non-virtuous actions, which are the main cause of all our suffering. If we do not cultivate a good heart, our selfish motivation destroys harmony and good relationships with others. We have no peace, and no chance to gain pure happiness. Without inner peace, outer peace is impossible. If we do not maintain a peaceful state of mind, we are not happy even if we have ideal conditions. On the other hand, when our mind is peaceful, we are happy, even if our external conditions are unpleasant. Therefore, the development of these qualities is of utmost importance for our daily happiness.

Geshe Kelsang Gyatso, or "Geshe-la" as he is affectionately called by his students, has designed three special spiritual programmes for the systematic study and practice of Kadampa Buddhism that are especially suited to the modern world – the General Programme (GP), the Foundation Programme (FP), and the Teacher Training Programme (TTP).

GENERAL PROGRAMME

The General Programme provides a basic introduction to Buddhist view, meditation, and practice that is suitable for beginners. It also includes advanced teachings and practice from both Sutra and Tantra.

FOUNDATION PROGRAMME

The Foundation Programme provides an opportunity to deepen our understanding and experience of Buddhism through a systematic study of five texts:

1 *Joyful Path of Good Fortune* – a commentary to Atisha's Lamrim instructions, the stages of the path to enlightenment.
2 *Universal Compassion* – a commentary to Bodhisattva Chekhawa's *Training the Mind in Seven Points*.
3 *Heart of Wisdom* – a commentary to the *Heart Sutra*.
4 *Meaningful to Behold* – a commentary to Venerable Shantideva's *Guide to the Bodhisattva's Way of Life*.
5 *Understanding the Mind* – a detailed explanation of the mind, based on the works of the Buddhist scholars Dharmakirti and Dignaga.

The benefits of studying and practising these texts are as follows:

(1) *Joyful Path of Good Fortune* – we gain the ability to put all Buddha's teachings of both Sutra and Tantra into practice. We can easily make progress on, and complete, the stages of the path to the supreme happiness of enlightenment. From a practical point of view, Lamrim is the main body of Buddha's teachings, and the other teachings are like its limbs.

(2) *Universal Compassion* – we gain the ability to integrate Buddha's teachings into our daily life and solve all our human problems.

(3) *Heart of Wisdom* – we gain a realization of the ultimate nature of reality. By gaining this realization, we can eliminate the ignorance of self-grasping, which is the root of all our suffering.

(4) *Meaningful to Behold* – we transform our daily activities into the Bodhisattva's way of life, thereby making every moment of our human life meaningful.

(5) *Understanding the Mind* – we understand the relationship between our mind and its external objects. If we understand that objects depend upon the subjective mind, we can change the way objects appear to us by changing our own mind. Gradually, we will gain the ability to control our mind and in this way solve all our problems.

TEACHER TRAINING PROGRAMME

The Teacher Training Programme is designed for people who wish to train as authentic Dharma Teachers. In addition to completing the study of twelve texts of Sutra and Tantra, which include the five texts mentioned above, the student is required to observe certain commitments with regard to behaviour and way of life, and to complete a number of meditation retreats.

All Kadampa Buddhist Centres are open to the public. Every year we celebrate Festivals in the USA and Europe, including two in England, where people gather from around the world to receive special teachings and empowerments and to enjoy a spiritual vacation. Please feel free to visit us at any time!

For further information, please contact:

UK NKT Office
Conishead Priory
Ulverston
Cumbria, LA12 9QQ
England

Tel/Fax: 01229-588533

Email: kadampa@dircon.co.uk
Website: www.kadampa.org

or

US NKT Office
Kadampa Meditation Center
47 Sweeney Road
P.O. Box 447
Glen Spey, NY 12737
USA

Tel: 845-856-9000
Fax: 845-856-2110

Email: info@kadampacenter.org
Website: www.kadampacenter.org

BOOKS OF RELATED INTEREST FROM NAB

A COMPLETE GUIDE TO MANAGING STRESS
—Dr. Bimal Chhajer
A Book by medical cardiologist who treats heart patients by stress managment, meditation, diet and exercises. It comes the scientific basis of stress, its origin practice solutions and communication skills. The whole book is practical and everyone can use it.

ISBN: 978-81-7822-186-1

9 SECRETS OF SUCCESSFUL MEDITATION
—Samprasad Dhundiraj Vinod
Yogi Dr. Vinod brings a fresh approach to Meditation; he inspires his readers to experience Meditation and to integrate it with their daily living; only those who really enjoy Meditation will do it regularly and thus get the most benefit from it. He shows the reader how to develop a true taste for Meditation, to take pleasure in it and thus to trigger spiritual growth and harmony in daily living.

ISBN: 978-81-7822-137-3

EXPLORING MEDITATION: Master the Ancient Art of Relaxation and Enlightenment—*Susan G. Shumsky*
This spiritual self-help book offers easy, step-by-step procedures to master the ancient arts of meditation and enlightenment. It offers practical techniques to increase love, power, and energy; reduce stress and tension; improve health; reverse aging; and bring well-being, and peace of mind to everyday life. This book demystifies abstract concepts and provides a road map to the inner life, leading beginners safely through the maze of the spiritual path, pointing out signposts and pitfalls along the way.

ISBN: 978-81-7822-296-7

GETTING TO WHERE YOU ARE: The Life of Meditation
—Steven Harrison
A penetrating and wide-ranging jouney through spirituality, meditation technology, and post-modern culture, *Getting to Where You Are* challenges the very basis of contemporary spirituality and the consumer society that created it. Steven Harrison explores what meditation actually is, and more importantly, what it is not, and how it got that way. In a direct and irreverent style, this one-of-a-kind spirituality book invites us all along for the ride, the twist and turns—and the final collision with life itself.

ISBN: 978-81-7822-202-8